DEVON AND CORNWALL

DEVON AND CORNWALL

RONALD DUNCAN

B T BATSFORD LTD LONDON

First published 1966

© Ronald Duncan 1966

MADE AND PRINTED IN GREAT BRITAIN
BY WILLIAM CLOWES AND SONS LTD, LONDON AND BECCLES
FOR THE PUBLISHERS B T BATSFORD LTD
4 FITZHARDINGE STREET, PORTMAN SQUARE, LONDON WI

CONTENTS

ACKNOWLEDGMENT

The Author and Publishers wish to thank the following for permission to reproduce the illustrations appearing in this book:

G. Douglas Bolton for figs. 4, 17 and 31
J. Allan Cash for figs. 8, 9, 12, 14, 21, 22 and 25
Leonard and Marjorie Gayton for figs. 7, 15, 20, 27 and 29
Noel Habgood for figs. 1, 3, 6, 11, 16, 18 and 23
A. F. Kersting for figs. 5 and 24
Kenneth Scowen for figs. 2, 13, 19 and 30
Geoffrey Shakerley for figs. 10, 26 and 28

DEVON AND CORNWALL

ATLANTIC

OCEAN

LUNDY ISLAND

Hartland Pt.
CLOVEL
HARTLAND

MORWENSTOW
KILKHAMPTON
STRATTON
BRA WORT

Bude

HOLSWORT

10

POUNDSTOCK

BOSCASTLE

TINTAGEL
DELABOLE

CAMELFORD

LAUNCESTON

Trevose Hd.

Bodmin Moor

PADSTOW

WADEBRIDGE

ST. CLEER

LANHYDROCK

CHAPTER

CHAPTER

NEW CHAPTER

CHAPTER

8

Newquay

PERRANPORTH

FOWEY
LOOE
POLPERRO

St. Austell
PROBUS
MEVAGISSEY

Gribbin Hd.

Truro

REDRUTH
CAMBORNE

Dodman Pt.

ST. IVES

ST. MARTIN'S

ST. MARY'S

SCILLY ISLES

Penzance
ST. MICHAEL'S MOUNT
NEWLYN
MOUSEHOLE
LAND'S END

Falmouth

ENGL

Lizard Point

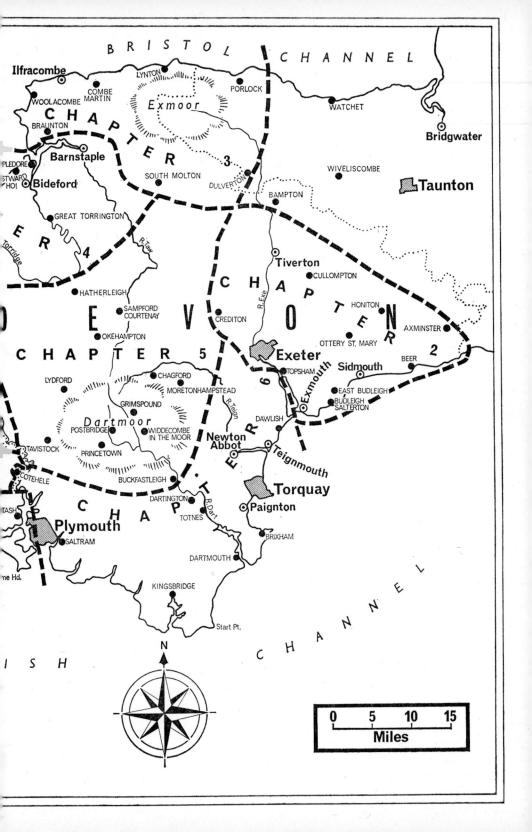

THE ILLUSTRATIONS

The Illustrations

ONE

Some Characteristics

If you can choose the time of the year to tour Devon and Cornwall, I would suggest the spring or the autumn. Try and avoid the summer, by which I mean late June, July and August. These months don't guarantee more sun in Devon—July and August have always been our wettest months. And the only reason why the tourists come to Devon then for their holidays is because of the school vacations. If you can come in the spring—April, May, or early June, you will see the country-side at its freshest. There will be primroses, lenten lilies and foxgloves in the hedge, whereas in August you will find only litter, blowing between the lay-bys and caravans. If you can't manage the spring, choose the autumn; after being in Devon for over 30 years I can assure you that October is our sunniest month. It is called St Luke's Little Summer. There are, of course, no wild flowers then, but the colours of the trees and the bracken on the moors are just as beautiful.

But spring is the best time of all to come here. May is the month for optimism, when every garden shouts with colours and even the gateposts blossom with promise.

The wild flowers of Devon make us easily the richest county in England. It is a Fort Knox of primroses. I know of valleys in the county where it is quite impossible to walk without treading upon these modest flowers. Similarly we have woods and coombes where the blue-bells enamel the ground thick enough to scythe. And after these, there are the great foxgloves keeping sentinel in the hedge, to be followed by the honeysuckle, perhaps the best of scents except for white jasmine or the Spanish flower, Lady of the Night.

And in addition to these we have more violets than you believed grew, and everywhere a romp of campions and many other little flowers of which I never know the name. A naturalist I met in North Devon last year told me he had found over 100 species of wild flowers, one of which he had believed to be extinct in England. People think of orchids as something rare; my cows graze on them here. And a wild orchis is prettier and less flamboyant than the cultivated thing.

If you do visit Devon and Cornwall during May and enjoy its squander of wild flowers, then you must try and return in October, for then the West Country is an entirely different place: the tawny bracken, beech hedges and hills of ling and heather paint a completely different landscape for you.

Has Devonshire any entity as a geographical or cultural unit? In what way does it differ from any other county? Its boundaries are marked on the map, but are they merely a convenience of county government, or do they delineate any geographical feature?

Like most geographical units, Devonshire is defined by rivers, such as the Teign, the Exe, the Tamar and the Torridge, which drain the uplands of Dartmoor and Exmoor. These are precisely the sort of natural boundaries which give a place and its people a real claim to a distinct cultural unity. The boundaries were not formed by accident, but by the elements. Indeed, Devonshire has more claim to its identity in this respect than many European countries. The present tendency in government and culture is towards centralisation and uniformity, and I suppose that some day such local boundaries will be of little but historic interest.

However, today, motoring from Seaton to Lynton, you know almost to within a mile when you have crossed the border of Somerset; and similarly going from Bideford to Bude, you know immediately you are in Cornwall. It is not only a question of seeing the more spacious parklands of Somerset give way to the pocket-handkerchief fields of Devon, or of noticing the ordered orchards break down to the ancient unpruned trees covered with old man's beard. It is not one particular thing which gives you the feeling that you are now in a different county, but many small details which you do not notice by themselves. Perhaps Somerset gates are differently shaped to Devon gates; each county of

2 Postbridge on Dartmoor

England has such idiosyncrasies, though iron gates are now reducing them to conformity.

The Cornish road is smooth compared to the Devon corrugated switchback; no signpost is necessary to mark the boundary between Devon and Cornwall: the bump on the tarmac is sufficient.

People are most easily defined by describing their dissimilarities, though the reason for such differences seems to defy explanation. Why is it that within two miles of the Devon–Somerset boundary you will hear a marked broadening of the vowel as you go west? There are as many definite dialects as there are counties in England, and even these are subdivided. People are very much as they speak; when their dialects differ it is almost certain that character does too. Devonshire will exist as a cultural unit with characteristics of its own just as long as the Devon dialect is still spoken.

There is another characteristic, peculiar to the county: as everybody knows, Devonians whitewash their farmhouses and cottages every spring. But it seems that nobody has the faintest idea why they do it. After all, it is an odd thing to do: no other county in the entire country finds it necessary to whiten all its walls and outhouses every April. And it is even stranger when you consider that Devon is the one county without a single lime-pit of its own. Every spring, they splash hundreds of tons of lime over their dwellings and over themselves and all of it has to be dragged here from Wiltshire or Hampshire. It is as odd and perverse for them to use lime as it would be if the people of Suffolk were to indulge in an annual rite of daubing their homes with a sticky veneer of Devon clay.

The origin of this annual ritual of whitewashing houses with lime (and many chapels too) derives from pagan mythology. It was believed that Pan would be frightened off by anything white. Subsequently, of course, the Christians insisted that white was holy.

I am looking at the character and the habits of the Devonians rather closely for I maintain that he who knows only the scenery of Devon knows little of the county. It is the people who make one place essentially different from another; and I am trying to understand why it is that I have chosen to live amongst the Devonians, when now that I come to think of it they seem to lack some of the virtues and many of

3 St. Michael's Mount seen from Marazion

the vices which I like to have around me. Staying with friends one seeks to compliment one's host; so living in Devonshire I would like to be able to flatter the Devonians. I would like to be able, for instance, to confirm the myth concerning the existence of Devon milkmaids of rare beauty; but I have not found many, after 30 years' residence in the county. If a girl has any looks, she takes them to where they will be better appreciated. The myth of rural beauty comes, of course, from the fact that women in towns commonly lost their complexions through the small-pox, whereas those in the country were spared.

All the talk that the rural population could be made to stay in the country by the installation of water closets and similar necessary but prosaic amenities was all very well; but depopulation of the villages has continued to prove that we have to give the country other things, perhaps not material, before the young people will stay there: not sanitary engineering, but useless carnivals, uneconomic enjoyment, a social devilment: an outlet for the spirit which can out of pleasure make a prayer.

Devon villages, like so many elsewhere, are fast becoming the mere repositories for the retired classes, where no entertainment is to be found other than an energetic game of bowls, and the morbid country habit of attending auction sales.

I hope I do not give the impression that I do not admire the Devonian, although perhaps one of their characteristics that most impresses me is common to all country people. I am thinking of their emotional stability. They have a kind of toughness which it would be wrong to dismiss as lack of emotion.

There is an old carpenter living near me in a small cottage a mile from any neighbour. He is now 84; his wife died when he was 60. For the last 24 years he has lived completely alone in his cottage, with only a weekly visit from his daughter, who comes out on the bus from Bideford, to look forward to. His eyes are too weak for him to read; he has not the strength to do much gardening, yet somehow he manages to keep his cottage clean and tidy, and what is stranger still, he never complains of the loneliness, although he must suffer from it. One would think that such people, and there are many even in my district, without anyone to look after them and without anything to look forward to would be driven to some kind of excess or eccentricity. But somehow they manage to preserve a balance which is lacking in more intelligent people.

I have often been fascinated by this quality and find that at the bottom of it lies a kind of self-respect. An example is the bachelor postman who does a ten-mile round every day to return to an empty cottage to get his own dinner; yet he always appears on a Sunday with his trousers creased and a flower in his buttonhole.

Whatever the roots of regional characteristics, they are not superficial. During the war when some American forces were quartered in the neighbourhood, I observed that traces of the connection between the Plymouth sailors who had accompanied the Pilgrim Fathers, and their descendants in the U.S. Army Air Force, had survived three centuries and 6,000 miles. These Americans discovered, to their amazement, that many Devon yokels were, as they put it, 'talking like Yanks'. They felt themselves flattered by imitation: whereas every time they said 'I guess', or 'I reckon', and many similar Americanisms, they were betraying the fact that the *Mayflower* sailed from Plymouth with a local crew. Most of the passengers on the *Mayflower* came from Norfolk via Holland, but the Plymouth sailors seem to have been more prolific.

The two fundamental factors which govern the character of a people are: first, their depth of soil, and secondly, their prevailing weather. I suspect the clipped vowels, the thrift and the canniness of the Scots is derived from the fact that in the Highlands the granite almost protrudes through the soil; and conversely in Devonshire, where we sit (apart from Dartmoor) on almost a foot of rich red loam and enjoy—or shall we say suffer?—a regular rainfall and a clement temperature, you find a broader vowel and a less energetic temperament. You may find meanness, but that is not thrift.

No other county in England has been endowed with such variety or fertility. The Devonian does not scrape a living from the soil; he milks nature as if she were a cow. What he plants will grow with the minimum of cultivation, and as a direct consequence his character has become essentially casual. Indeed the thesis that the depth of soil determines the difference between the Devonians and the Scots can be established within Devonshire itself. The architecture, diet and the general way of life in the dour granite villages of Dartmoor bear a distinct resemblance to Aberdeenshire. As you climb from the shelter of Totnes up to the moorland, you will see the cottages change from whitewashed haphazard cob and thatch to careful granite blocks with slate roofs. The weather and the soil have made the change; and, on the moors where sheep farming is the only industry, you will find the iron griddle is used just as in Scotland, for shepherds can pack flat oatcakes into their haversacks more easily than lowland buns. On the other hand, sheltered coastal towns like Torquay or Teignmouth have acquired the name of Riviera; and they do in fact present certain Mediterranean characteristics.

One might think that in a county which was endowed with such fertile soil and clement weather, and where poverty is, if not completely unknown, at least inexcusable, the people would have almost a continental gaiety about them. Work in Devon is never unrewarded. You have only to plant to be assured of a harvest. Indeed, many Devonians appear to do no more than watch the grass grow. Yet why do they look so severe, turning their work into drudgery and their leisure into a mere loose end? They seem to have no excess in them, either for virtue or for vice. And why is it they so seldom sing? Is it that they are so spoiled by nature that they are bored by her? They tolerate this good fortune rather like a man who, married to a beautiful wife, is both faithful and indifferent.

One can understand perhaps why Scotland and the northern coasts of England lack the festive spirit. Carnivals and an east wind are incompatible. Yet how is it that Devon is almost entirely devoid of any traditional festivals?

The late Rev. Stephen Hawker, who was vicar of my local parish church 50 years ago, made a poet's effort to reintroduce the pagan festival of the harvest, and managed so successfully to graft it on to the Christian calendar that within a generation the Harvest Festival had spread over the entire country and across to America. But though the village altars are still loaded with obese marrows, strings of shallots, baskets of apples, and decorated with sheaves of wheat, even here in the very centre of its origin, the festival has become no more than a relic displayed in an empty church. It is not the joyous celebration of gratitude which Hawker wanted to revive.

Any excuse for a celebration is worthy of consideration. But whereas the Harvest Festival in pagan days was probably a matter of genuine joy, tacked on to our parish it merely became a fruit show on the altar. The reason for this decline is, I suppose, that the Devon farmer is so used to plenty that he takes cornucopia as his perquisite. He shows no gratitude, for he feels none. He shows no joy at a full harvest, for he so seldom experiences the disappointment of a poor one. The faith which once produced the intense fervour of a medieval Plough Sunday has entirely disappeared: though it is not, perhaps, that faith itself has evaporated, but that its object has been transferred. The Devon farmer, like his neighbours, now worships strange gods. In place of fertility myths, he believes in the use of certain well-advertised brands of chemical manure.

This is not the place to discuss the comparative merits of religions, but it would seem that the contemporary scientific belief has this to be said against it: that its dogma is grim, and its liturgy dull.

A vital community usually seizes on both the harvest and the marriage as excuses for celebration; and though there is no sign of anything like excessive pleasure shown when the corn is carried, one might still expect some festive spirit to burst the Wesleyan straitjacket on the occasion of a wedding.

A people's agriculture is the one thing they cannot possibly conceal: for you have only to travel a few miles by road or by rail to be able to read the pages of the fields which are laid open for you. And you do not have to go very far into Devon before two things strike you: the first is the generosity of nature, and the second is the meanness of man. Devon has been endowed with rich soil, good rainfall (average 30-40 inches a year), valleys, rivers and stock. But no sooner are you in the county than you notice a worsening of the pastures (one-quarter of Devon's land is rough pasture and moorland), a crumbling of the farm buildings and slovenliness in the hedges. Of course Devon farming has improved vastly in the last 20 years but it still lags behind a great deal of England.

Without any exaggeration, I would say Devon farming could support 3,000 Italian peasants without the Devon farmer having to give up a single rod of ground which he is now using. You may think that the scenery more than compensates for the appalling wastage of ground, but how is it that the Devonian wastes so much? I suppose the answer is that he can neglect the soil because he can live off the scenery. Only 15 per cent of the population work the land; only one per cent bother with fishing, but 66 per cent of the working population are in 'service' jobs in the towns (public works, commerce, entertainment and domestic service), whose main task is to serve the visitors and retired classes; and they make enough during the summer to live fairly comfortably in the winter.

I am aware that I am running counter to tradition in descrying Devon as an agricultural county, for it is known as a land of milk and honey. The truth is that there is plenty of milk but precious little honey; for it is easier for the Devonian to feed his visitors on canned goods than produce from the fields that lie outside his door. He does not even bother to grow one-hundredth part of the fruit he could, and even the famous Devonshire cider presses now have to import apple pulp from neighbouring counties, because local orchards are of little use other than support for clothes lines. The economy of many Devon smallholders is, indeed, based very largely on taking summer visitors. They look upon this as their best harvest.

Even so, in spite of all the casual methods employed, they are harvesting corn in the village this year, and the average yield per acre is between 40 and 50 bushels, compared to the average American yield of 18 bushels per acre. At least the Devonian has not raped his soil— he has not exploited it into a dust bowl; all the fertility has not been converted into cash, as in the U.S.A.; nor has he cut all his timber for firewood till the hillsides are washed of their topsoil. Devon is still fertile.

So much for the economics of farming; and looking round at the Devon smallholdings, with their divided and intermixed fields, and observing many of their antiquated methods, a visitor is tempted to make all sorts of suggestions for the rationalisation of cultivation and specialisation in crops. But it may well be that the so-called efficiency which might be imposed on them would in the long run do more harm than good. The Devon smallholder with his mixed farming, which looks so inefficient, may provide just that kind of modest succouring which the land requires, and were we to turn him into a specialist producer, it is quite possible that the land would eventually leave him on a gust of wind, or he leave the land.

Fertility is not a thing to tamper with; and corn crops without rotation could leech it all away. But this extreme exploitation of the soil can hardly take place in Devonshire; the land is too broken to support prairie farming, yet, were we to try and make the Devon smallholder more of a specialist and a skilled man, and less of a handyman, we might find we had produced a person who was far too impatient to bother with such fertile but diminutive fields.

The Devonian farm-hand resists any kind of innovation and his attitude to improvement is often one of profound contempt. By temperament and habit he is what is now known as a subsistence smallholder. That is to say he tends not to show much interest in getting from the land more than he requires for his immediate needs. He has other resistances too.

What does he do if his chimney stack is blown off in a gale? Does he first 'phone up a builder's merchant for a new one? No; that is the last thing he does. He takes a glance round his farmyard to see what is lying around that might possibly be made to do the job. He sees an old earthenware bread crock, which he borrowed from his wife's kitchen months ago to use as a milk bucket after a lorry had run over his own . . . with a few deft taps of a hammer he knocks the bottom out and proudly hoists it up on to the roof to serve as a chimney, which it has done adequately for as long as I can remember, until ivy has grown over it, and it looks so much in keeping with the rest of the roof that no one ever notices it.

And as you travel through Devon you observe innumerable examples of this ability to make do, or as the Devonians aptly put it, 'to fake up'. You will see old bedsteads stuffing the gaps in hedges, or a pair of harrows on their edges used as a trellis for climbing beans, and I dare say if you're near the coast, either in South or North Devon, you will see several ships' wheels, which have either been turned on their sides and used as tables, or slung from a couple of hooks to swing as a gate.

I often call Devon and Cornwall Depressed Areas; and they are extremely poor in artistic activities. Compared to Bali, they are Backward Areas too. Why should material wealth be the only measurement for prosperity? Towns as large as Exeter and Barnstaple are without a theatre. You will wonder if Cromwell is still alive or whether we keep a perpetual but un-Christian Lent. You might suspect its interests had gone into more homely pursuits. In the country districts of France there is very little interest in the arts, but the cheese and the wine they make there perhaps give the people more right to be called cultured than if they were all poetasters and opera singers.

Devon has little music, less poetry, neither an opera house nor a theatre. So it should have its gastronomic specialities; but, for the most part, they are only distant memories.

One rainy day a few years ago I unearthed an old map of the West Country which had fallen behind a drawer of my desk. I had never seen it before; probably it belonged to the former owner of the desk. It was more of a picture than a map. Silver trout leapt out of little streams; salmon were shown in the Torridge estuary, and wherever a pond or lake occurred carp were depicted in them. It was an epicure's map drawn, I guess, by some eighteenth-century traveller who had stopped at each village and recorded the particular product of each with a little drawing.

Some villages had a cask of cider superimposed over their name or crest; others had barrels of beer; one or two, a flagon of wine. A few had an illustration of a flitch of bacon or a haunch of venison. I observed that this traveller had tasted 28 different varieties of cheese in Devon alone, each being the proud and particular delicacy of a locality. I noticed too that Weare Gifford had once been famous for strawberries, and that Exeter had a greater claim to repute on account of its melons than its cathedral. I looked at my own village to see if we had any claim to be on the map, and was gratified to see a small biscuit barrel drawn on the neighbouring Bursdon Moor.

I wondered how many of the 28 different cheeses were still made. I guessed that even their recipes had been long forgotten and the presses broken; and for a few moments I meditated the tastes I would never know, wondering whether there had once been a Devon Brie, and how many nuances of Stilton. But I awoke from this succulent reverie to be called in to supper: there stood the white loaf, the Pan-American cheese and the International butter; and to console myself I drank the same brand of beer that crofters in the Shetlands, and gold-diggers in Australia, and perhaps even Lamas in Tibet would be tasting, and I cursed the uniformity that reduces us to the dullness of processed Cheddar. It was bad enough when we excused uniformity on the grounds that it was an economic expedient, but now it is worse; we think the expedient is an end in itself.

One still sees the notice 'Devonshire Cream Teas' outside every farmhouse on the road, though this delicacy may not survive our age which confuses fashion with taste. At least it will survive in isolated farms in my neighbourhood, where the farms keep a few Devon cows which, in spite of their poor yield of milk, produce a fairly high butter-fat content, largely due to the amount of yarrow indigenous to the pastures. And even though most farms have turned to milk production because it brings in a monthly cash return, the milk from one cow is still kept for the house.

The milk is set in shallow enamel pans to stand in the cool for 12 hours, after which the farmer's wife gently lifts the pan on to her kitchen range and heats it slowly without letting it boil. She waits until the shape of the bottom of the pan is outlined in the cream on the surface as a circle concentric to the rim. The cream is now scalded. She then removes the pan gently back to the cool dairy, which is generally shelved with Delabole slates from Cornwall, and there she leaves it to stand for another 12 hours. The cream is then taken off with a fish slice, and the skimmed milk that is left fed to the pigs or calves.

I have often given this recipe to friends who had farms in other parts of the country, and they have often tried it, but though their cream had the right consistency about it, it lacked the peculiar flavour which makes Devonshire cream so unique. I believe I have found the secret of this flavour. One friend of mine who owned a small herd of Ayrshires in Wiltshire kept a modern concrete and tubular steel shippon with a

T.T. chromium-plated dairy adjoining could not get anywhere with
the recipe until eventually I sent him an old dung-covered bucket from
a typical Devon shippon. He hung this in his dairy and within a few
days had achieved the identical flavour in his cream. It would seem the
bacteria on the bucket were a necessary part, which is not surprising,
for something similar was experienced in modern factories which tried
vainly to make old cheeses. Eventually they had to incorporate the
plaster from an old cheese factory into their new walls. There is, of
course, a wholly underdeveloped industry here, for Devonshire cream
is the one product of the county which has a universal name. It would
enable them to keep all the skim milk on their farms which, fed to
pigs, would mean that some fertility was kept on their holdings;
whereas now all goes off in the churns, gradually leeching the farm of
its lime and phosphates.

But in spite of (or because of) her supplies of eggs, cream and butter,
the Devon housewife is not a cook. She is rather a builder, who believes
in laying a solid foundation to the day at breakfast, and a secure tombstone over it of an evening. She is a great believer in pastry, and provides
her family with soggy waistcoats of pastry to keep out one wind, and
generate another.

The dough does not lack good ingredients—she is very lavish with
fresh butter—nor energy in the mixing. The trouble, I believe, comes
from this profligate use of cream, which is not only mixed generously
with the filling of the pastry, but thickly basted over the lid before
putting in the oven. Not even the best of dough can resist this treatment. The commonest filling for these impervious pasties is potato,
sliced, with parsley and covered with cream. Parsley with egg, and
even parsley on its own are also favoured.

Even along the coast, many Devonians believe that shellfish is unfit
to eat: I have often been warned not to eat lobsters because 'they be
poison'. However, if you dig over any garden within three miles of
the coast in North Devon, you will find as many limpet shells as stones;
before the smallholders could depend on tourist traffic, they were
grateful for this harvest from the rocks, and would mince the limpets
up and bury them in a pasty. But I do not suppose a single limpet has
been cooked in Devonshire for many years, except for a most un-

successful experiment I recently made in pickling them. I also eat them raw, like oysters.

Strangely enough, although the Devon housewife restricts her choice of vegetables to the most obvious varieties, and forbears eating any but the most well-known kinds of fish, a few will still go down to the rocks with an old pail and gather laver. This is a kind of seaweed, generally called black butter, but pale green in colour when gathered. She prepares this by leaving it to soak for a few hours, then boiling it for four or five, changing the water several times. She drains the brew, and the remaining black butter is then fried and served with bacon. The liquid that has been drained off will set almost solid when cooled, and it contains a very high proportion of iodine. It is usually thrown away, although it is probably more nourishing than the part that is eaten. Laver is a little slimy to the palate, but this quality can be overcome by a squeeze of lemon juice, which makes it delightful to eat. It is said to be a mild laxative. It is strange that the gathering and eating of laver should have persisted when the use of other wild foods has been forgotten.

Many farms still make their own cider. I had an intimate initiation into this beverage some years ago when visiting a tenant near Tiverton. Having missed my train, I did not arrive until it was almost dark. However, the farmer was most insistent that I should walk over the farm with him, and examine his stock and crops. He was a very good farmer and proud of his sheep, and I hesitated to suggest that as it was now so dark I should be unable to see very much. 'You don't need to see my sheep,' he exclaimed, 'just lay your hands on their backs.' And off he led me through fields of mangolds, kale and clover, each of which I had to appraise by running my hands through the wet crop, until we reached a gate about a mile and a half from the farm. His dog barked the sheep through, and upon each back I had to lay my hand. After another hour of trailing through cornfields, feeling for the ears of wheat, and finally grovelling to examine pigs in a pitch-dark sty, I was allowed to return to the old farm kitchen, where I was regaled with a mug of home-brewed cider as a fitting reward.

I would have concluded it was a practical joke if I had not just seen my host drink an equal quantity, for this beverage was too strong for hospitality.

The next morning, with all the nausea of a hangover, I had to breathe the fumes arising from a vast vat of cider in an old barn, where giant wooden rollers pulped the apples. The farmer told me that there was nothing gave cider that extra kick so well as a haunch of meat thrown into the cask and left there to decompose. I believed him, and looking round at the rat runs, wondered whether any dissolved rodents had contributed to my splitting head.

Apparently the old man had often helped to brew, so I asked him to come to my farm and help me make some beer in the cauldron, and abandoned all thoughts of using it for a log basket. After some difficulty he remembered how it used to be done.

First he took two bushels of barley, which he damped down and spread on the barn floor. He left it there until the grain had swollen and the little shoots had almost appeared; then with a wooden shovel he turned it in order to dry it off quickly. This crude process makes malt. After making his malt he cleaned out an old wooden tub, which stood underneath my swede cutter. He poured the malt into this, then added 20 gallons of water. He let this stand and work for 48 hours, poured the liquid into the copper cauldron and added five ounces of hops and four ounces of yeast. Finally he heated the cauldron on a slow fire for 24 hours, taking great care not to let it boil.

When the beer had brewed, he poured it into a barrel, and added another 20 gallons of water to the original malt in the wooden tub, let it stand as before, strained it and then put it over the fire. Thus he made nearly 40 gallons of beer from two bushels of barley.

The first brewing produced what is called audit ale, which used to be found in some college cellars. It was bottled under the name of barley wine and bore five crosses on the label. The other 20 gallons was an ordinary strong ale. The barrels were only lightly bunged whilst the beer was working. Finally it was cleared with a little isinglass.

Years ago farmers were allowed to brew beer up to the value of their annual rent; now both the permission and the knowledge are lacking. A bushel of barley costs about 15/-, and it would seem that Devonians might find home-brewed beer very much cheaper than the ersatz stuff they buy. Why have they ceased to brew? I suspect for two reasons:

firstly, they have forgotten the recipe, secondly, they will never be bothered to make the best if they can buy the second best.

After all, how many Devon housewives bake bread? Although a few still make the delicious 'cut rounds', as they are called in North Devon, or 'splits' in South Devon, and these are in fact no more than yeast rolls, made in exactly the same way as bread.

Another speciality that still survives is ammonia biscuit. It is strange to find these on the same table with the lumpen unimaginative pasties; for these ammonia biscuits are as good as Bath Olivers.

I have often watched them made. Rub six ounces of butter or cream (generally the latter) into one pound of flour. Add six ounces of sugar. Beat an egg with a little milk and a teaspoonful of bicarbonate of ammonia dissolved in it. Then mix liquid with solids to make a stiff dough. Roll out very thin and cut into rounds with an inverted tumbler. Bake biscuits on greased tins in a moderate oven till they are a light brown. A richer variant, quite extinct now, followed the same recipe, but four eggs were used and the mixture was bound together with white wine instead of milk.

I discovered another recipe when I was given a delicious piece of cake at a lifeboat station in a fishing village on the south coast. I asked the old man how it was made, and through the noise of the gale he told me.

'You take a bottle of rum and pour some over a pound of dried figs. When the figs have swollen up till they be as plump as toads, you take some splits, cut them in two and slap a fig between each.'

'What do you do then,' I asked, 'to get such a delicious cake?'

'Why, you just put one in your hip pocket before you go out in the boat, and as you row the motion of your backside so squeezes the nature of the fig and the rum into the split, that ye have the cake ye're eating.'

Yet it can't be the cooking which keeps me in Devon. Whether the puritans have made the diet, or the diet has made them puritans, I don't know. At its best the food is wholesome, but that word never described good cooking.

Now can I persuade myself that I live in Devon because it is in any sense a centre of culture—using the word in the accepted sense?

There are only two theatres in the entire county. It is absolutely no exaggeration to say that the average Devonian has never seen a live play, and what is worse, does not regret the matter. Since we lack a repertory company of our own, occasional optimistic groups will visit one of the seaside towns in the summer season; but this is theatre for the tourists, and the Devonian proper shows no interest, and gives little encouragement, not having the time.

As to music, the Devonian is content with the harmonium's bronchial wheezing. Music, to him, must be sacred, and he believes that which is sacred must be dull. He takes his art as he takes religion—as a purgative. There are few orchestras in the entire county, and I do not think more than two or three music clubs. I used to know an old miller who lived alone in a cottage near me, who of an evening took up an old fiddle and tuned the strings of the instrument he kept in the chimney so that they were mellowed by the smoke; and I heard him on countless evenings playing away to himself. But this is an exception. I do not suppose there are 50 fiddles in the whole of Devonshire, or five in Cornwall.

All of which makes one wonder what is the relationship between 'literacy' or 'culture' and the land.

There is at the moment a move to spread culture from London through the small towns even to the remotest Devon and Cornish villages. The Arts Council are doing their utmost to support drama and music in the country. No doubt all this is most commendable, and within another generation I will have a carpenter who will be able to quote me passages from Dante and discuss the wastes of the Russian novel; and then we shall be so cultured we shall be able to sit on a chair which will break and which neither of us can mend, under a roof which leaks and neither of us can thatch.

But I doubt it. The Devonian is too sure of himself to allow himself to be altered. He is indifferent to criticism, insulated against education. He does not want to be improved for he is quite certain he is perfect. Perhaps he is.

I have wondered why the farmers around me are so indifferent to anything which is not essentially an immediate, practical matter. I

4 *Sidmouth: a rare run of unspoiled cliff*

have suggested that this is because they have little time for anything else and perhaps due to the fact that since farming satisfies the spirit a farmer needs no separate spiritual expression. But I doubt whether this explanation is sufficient to cover the Devonian's self-confidence which he shows when faced by any human experience of his own, or the boredom which he does not even trouble to hide when confronted with the experiences of others. He does not listen to music. He seldom reads. I do not suppose that more than a dozen books of poetry are read each month in the whole county. Is it that the Devonian is deaf, is it that he cannot read? It is that he has no need. He is self-sufficient.

One cannot help but admire such equanimity of temperament. Sometimes one is amused by it. I am thinking of an old farm labourer I knew who lost his wife during the spring about ten years ago. I was surprised to see the old man weeping openly as he followed the coffin to the churchyard. This was the first time I had seen grief shown in Devon and I wondered then how often it remained hidden by superficial restraint. A week later I was gratified in a sentimental way to see the old man tending his wife's grave. I noticed he was planting it out with bulbs. But as I saw later they were not daffodils but shallots! It was not possible that he had mistaken one plant for another. I challenged him. He replied, looking down at the grave, 'It seemed such a pity to waste that bit of ground.' And I was forced to wonder whether onions had not also produced his tears as well as consoled his grief.

Another thing which keeps these people on an even keel is a sense of economy. I do not suggest that they are mean, but they cannot bear to see any kind of waste, and it is for this reason that the postman's shoes are kept well dubbined and his garden free of weeds.

Many of these people suffer a kind of inarticulate and unsensational martyrdom. Sometimes I have wondered whether or not their inability to express their emotions has meant that they are incapable of feeling them, but this is not the case.

5 *Lantic Bay, Cornwall*

TWO

Exeter and East Devon

Assuming you can only spend a fortnight in the West Country, I suggest you spend two nights centred in Exeter. You could stay at the 'Clarence' where you would certainly enjoy the atmosphere of the Cathedral Close. From there, with Exeter as a centre, spend one day going to East Devon, Honiton and Axminster; another for Budleigh Salterton, Ottery St Mary; and then the third day could take you in the direction of Exmoor via Crediton and Tiverton.

Next I suggest you base yourself on Exmoor for at least two days. You can stay at the 'Poltimore Arms', the 'Doone Valley Hotel' or at Exford. You will need at least two days to get the feel of Exmoor and I think you will enjoy these as much as any.

In North Devon I suggest you base yourself at 'Tanton's Hotel' in Bideford. It is opposite the river, and you will enjoy watching the men fishing from the bridge or pulling in their nylon nets beneath it.

In North Devon you will need at least three days. A week has already gone. A fortnight is not long enough. Especially since any visitor to the West Country will want to spend at least two days on Dartmoor. I recommend the 'Three Crowns Hotel' in Chagford. And then you still have South Devon. You will have to manage this in three days, which gives you two days left for Cornwall. But you see, it is quite impossible: you will just have to stay for three weeks.

By allocating two weeks for Devonshire and one week for Cornwall I am not being biased in any way. As a matter of fact my farm is in both counties, and so I can claim allegiance to whichever county I like—and be disclaimed by both. The fact is Devon is very much larger than Cornwall. I could say that in my opinion it is the more beautiful of the two, but I do not think that would mean very much, for you cannot compare them: they are different.

The history of Devon and Cornwall might be said to be lost within a number of bad books. Most original research is of recent date. What the historians have done one can see by comparing their works, for they have merely quoted and misquoted each other, and made a book without making an effort. But this is not the place for me to rectify their omissions even if I had the scholarship with which to do so.

But it is impossible to get in a picture of a place without some regard to its past. Devon has the oldest past in England. Not only are there innumerable traces of Iron Age and Bronze Age Settlements but of several palaeolithic and neolithic periods.

After these last two come the barrow builders, of which there are many traces in both Devon and Cornwall. These round tumuli are distinct from the long barrows which can be seen in Dorset and Wiltshire and seem to indicate that a separate race lived in the peninsula. An indication of the ancient history of this area can be gauged from the fact that tin-mining was carried on at Carnon and at Pentaun at a time when the mammoth still existed in the West of England and when the general level of the two counties was about 30 feet higher than it is now. Whatever the Bronze Age was, it originated in this corner of England where metal was mined. The whole period has been neglected. We have spent more time in Egyptian research than we have in unearthing our own history.

The assumption that no civilisation existed in this part of the world until the Romans reached here does not bear the most casual scrutiny. Indeed, it may have been the existence of a Celtic civilisation that caused the Romans to restrain their colonisation in this part of the world. At that time, Devon and Cornwall were not separated but made up one country, the Kingdom of Dunmonia. There is no evidence that this Kingdom was ever conquered by the Romans, and it has been suggested that it retained its independence throughout the occupation under its own ruler. There are few sites west of Exeter, which of course was a Roman citadel, to indicate that the rest of the country was occupied. Only a few towns such as Scobchester and Wickchester indicate their occupation, and at Emary Beacon, which is situated between the cliffs of Welcombe and Hartland, there are unmistakable traces of a Roman Fosse.

The wholly inadequate evidence for the history of this part of England is so obscure that it is impossible to make any definite statements: the only source of the Saxon record is the *Chronicle*, which does not go further back than the eighth century.

William of Malmesbury reported that Synewulf (755-784), the King of Wessex, conquered most of Devon and Cornwall. And he states that the Britons were driven out of Exeter in 926, back to the Tamar. The full extent of the Saxon occupation of the old Celtic kingdom can now be gauged from the towns with the Saxon endings, 'worthy', 'cot', 'hay'. As late as Domesday the population of Devon was no higher than 17,000.

From the few stone works and carvings which can now be seen in Devon and Cornwall it seems that the Celtic civilisation of that period is one to which a great deal more attention should be given. Unhappily farmers, road-makers and bridge-builders have not made the archeaologists' nor the historians' work any easier by carrying off many Celtic monuments with which to make bridges or break up for roads. Only recently I myself discovered a granite gatepost near Jacobstow which had carvings of this period down one face.

The history of Exeter contains the history of England. The Romans most probably took over a Celtic town when they founded the city in A.D. 50. Subsequently the town was occupied by innumerable conquerors. The Danes in 876 laid siege to it and were eventually thrown out by Alfred. In 1003 it was captured by Swegen who sacked it and laid waste to the entire district. Under Edward the Confessor the city rose again, and the monastery was raised to the rank of a cathedral.

William the Conqueror was the next to assault the walls. The citizens replied: 'We will neither take any oath to the King or allow him to enter our city, but the tribute which, following ancient custom we were wont to give formally to another, the same we will give to him.'

Not satisfied with this the Conqueror laid siege to the town and eventually subdued it, and the Normans erected Rougemont Castle. Before the building was finished the Saxons tried to retake Exeter but were beaten off and destroyed in a battle on the bank of the Tavy. For the next few hundred years Exeter seems to have maintained its growth by the expediency of giving its loyalty to the winning side. It was Lancastrian at the time of the Wars of the Roses, and yet submitted to Edward IV.

> *When last I was at Exeter,*
> *The Mayor in courtesy showed me the castle,*
> *And called it Rougemont, at which name I started,*
> *Because a bard of Ireland told me once*
> *I should not live long after I saw Richmond.*

These lines from *Richard III* may appear to be a very bad pun, but in all probability the Elizabethan pronunciation of Rougemont may not have been all that dissimilar from Richmond.

Perkin Warbeck made Exeter his first object when he landed in Cornwall in 1497, and it was in this city that he was brought before the King in the Cathedral Close with a halter round his neck.

It is strange that, though Devonshire is one of the strongholds of Wesleyanism, yet Exeter, its county town, was the most active centre in England against the Reformation. The Western Rebellion was centred there, though unlike most rebellions, which are fermented in cities, this one was sustained by disaffection in the countryside. The Devonians' grudge was because the closure of 24 major religious houses in the county had impoverished them by the withdrawal of patronage in one form or another; and the countryman had also discovered to his dismay that the new landlords, such as the Russells at Tavistock, were very much less easy-going than the abbots had been. Land which they had been allowed previously to graze was suddenly enclosed or ploughed up. Rivers that they had fished, and woods from which they had drawn their firing, became protected by foresters and water bailiffs.

The Western Rebellion was based on popular economic resentment and not on dogmatic issues. It is hard to imagine the Devonian yokel taking up arms for anything as distant as the Trinity, though the substitution of the ordinary prayer-book service for the Mass did cause this resentment to break into violence. The Rebellion started at Sandford Court on the outskirts of Dartmoor. The parishioners forced the parish priest to wear his own old vestments and say Mass instead of the Church of England service. Other parishes followed their example. Cornwall and Somerset took up the movement, and several officers sent to suppress it were killed.

Crediton became the centre. Eventually, landlords like Sir Humphrey Arundel of Cornwall led the rebels, who with a force of 10,000 marched on Exeter, where the City refused to surrender. Siege was laid, and the Lord Lieutenant of the County opened negotiations. The rebels' terms were that Catholic worship should be restored; that the Bible should be called in before 'it makes more heretics'; that Cardinal Pole should be pardoned; and that some of the land sequestered from the Church should be returned to establish other religious houses.

The terms were refused. The authorities temporised until they could bring up forces of mercenaries, mainly Italian. The first battle was fought at Fenniton Bridge, and the rebels were routed at Woodbury. Their leaders were sent to London and, except for Sir Thomas Pomeroy, who lost his estates, they were all executed. Over 4000 Devonians were slaughtered. The Vicar of St Thomas's Church in Exeter was hanged in his vestments from his own church tower. The brutality of the times can be assessed by the fact that his body was left there until the accession of Mary.

At the Civil War, Exeter was quickly snapped up by the Russells and garrisoned for Parliament, but was taken by the Cavaliers, who made it one of their strongholds for the duration of the war, until it surrendered to General Fairfax in 1646.

It was one of the first cities to show loyalty to Charles II and to switch its allegiance to William of Orange, in line with its strategy of expediency, though the Dean and Chapter walked out of the Cathedral in front of the Prince when his Declaration was read before them.

I have recommended the 'Royal Clarence' partially because of the architecture around the hotel, and I do not only refer to the Cathedral itself. After Salisbury, Exeter precinct is one of the most elegant in the country. If you fail to take in any of my notes concerning the history of

Exeter, you will be quite unable to avoid the past when you stay at this hotel, because they have stained glass panes to the windows depicting various facets of the city's history: showing the Ancient Briton, the Dane and the Normans, including such figures as Agnes Preest, burned at the stake in 1558; and the Countess Isabel, who tried to cut off the river from the city when she constructed Countess Weir. Most rooms in the hotel are named after Devon worthies.

But though little of this historical background is visible, the Cathedral is a manifestation of it all. It is the finest example of symmetrical decorated Gothic in this country.

Personally I think Gothic architecture is at its best so much like a force of nature that it is beyond personal taste. Apart from minor renovations, some due to war damage when Exeter was bombed, the Cathedral stands now as it did in the fourteenth century. Of course, the first thing about it which will impress you is undoubtedly the fabulous West Front with its screen of statues of saints, apostles, martyrs and kings. The extraordinary thing about it is that although these are carved in stone, the overall effect is that of lightness. It is almost as though a fold of Honiton lace hung over the front. It is very beautiful, and you will wonder why funds are not found to stop the decay. Inside the Cathedral the roof cannot fail to be admired, also the Lady Chapel and the Choir Screen. The Bishop's throne carved out of oak will be, inevitably, pointed out to you, but though the workmanship which went into it must be admired, the overall design is too fussy, as are the carvings above the choir stalls restored by Sir Gilbert Scott.

The oldest collection of Anglo-Saxon poetry—*Codex Exoniensis*—exists in the Cathedral library and, as far as I know, has not yet been translated.

In the Close opposite Exeter Cathedral is the parish church of St Martin's, which often goes unnoticed, because attention is naturally directed to the Cathedral only 50 yards away. But this tiny church is worth particular attention. One record states it was dedicated in 1065. There may have been an earlier church on the same site founded by the Bishop of Tours, who died in 397. Most of the extant building dates from the fifteenth century. It is built of local stone and its design is simple. The roof is the original oak barrel-vaulted with moulded ribs

6 *Exeter Cathedral : the best example of*
ornamented Gothic

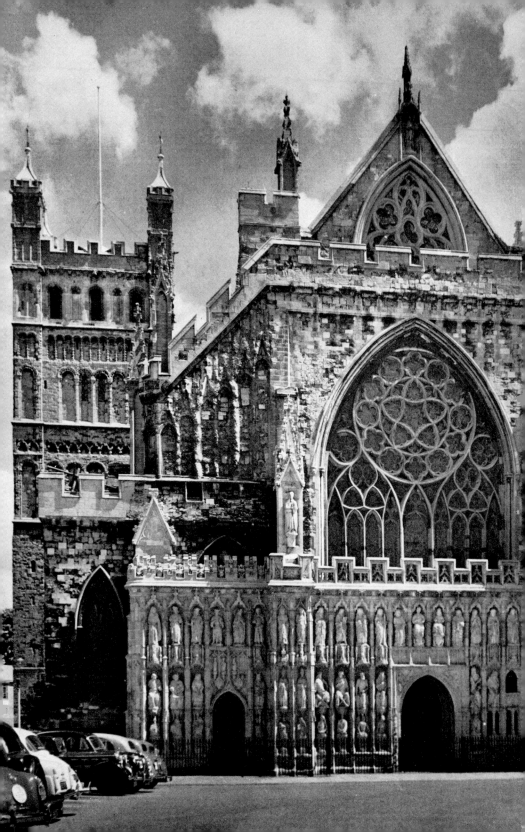

and carved bosses. The West window is fifteenth-century. A good deal of the woodwork is of the seventeenth. There is a fine Jacobean Communion Table. But it is not in any particular detail that this church achieves its elegant interior, but rather through its overall proportions. The church is small, which is appropriate, since its parish is less than $1\frac{3}{4}$ acres in extent.

And before you leave the Close you must look at the splendid Bishops' Palace which adjoins; and you will enjoy the shops around the Cathedral. There is a bookshop standing like an oasis in that desert of illiteracy which stretches from London to Land's End, in this so-called age of mass education; I discovered there are now fewer bookshops in Devonshire, Somerset and Cornwall than there are in the whole of Milan.

And do not fail to visit the delicatessen 50 yards from the Cathedral. You will need to fill up your picnic basket when you drive off into the puritanical regions of the hinterland where *Défense de Manger* might be an appropriate road sign.

Several old buildings in the city, such as Chevalier House, were destroyed in the air raids during the war, but St Martin's Church and Moll's Coffee House, where the Elizabethan sailors like Raleigh and Drake used to meet, still exist. Also, I recommend the walk along the quay in front of the 'Prospect Inn', where you can see the extremely finely proportioned Customs House, and behind it the old medieval street, Slepcote Hill, which is exactly as it was in the thirteenth century. St Nicholas' Priory, endowed before the Conquest, Tuckers' Hall and the Mint are also well worth seeing.

But it is possible to get the feel of Exeter more by wandering along the river banks looking at the swans, and visualising the ships which used to come in here and tie up when Exeter was a centre of the wool trade.

The city is, of course, no longer a centre of industry. It is sustained now by being a civic centre, and by the University which has grown up so rapidly during the last 20 years. It is probable that Exeter's future is as a university town.

Powderham Castle, on the main road road between Exeter and Dawlish, is of particular interest. It is still the home of the Earls of

Tiverton Church porch (1517)

Devon. The Courtenays have, over the last ten centuries, contributed more to the County's history than any other family. One could even say that the history of the Courtenays is almost the history of Devonshire. Amongst the many things within the house which are worth seeing, the music room, designed by Wyatt, is particularly distinguished. It also contains one of the finest seventeenth-century organs in the country.

When you leave Exeter, be sure to have a good road map in the car. And by that I don't mean one of those motoring handbooks which merely show only the main roads. You will need an Ordnance Survey map (sheet 15), scale a quarter-inch to the mile, which costs 7/6d. I repeat, if you want to see Devon and Cornwall, there is no point in keeping to the main roads. On these you will see nothing but traffic, and your only views will be of garages. The main roads of Devon are as ugly as any, and to keep to them is to proceed, but *not* to travel. On the average main road it is impossible to tell which county of England you are in. Consequently, as you may have come from some distance to see Devon, I am not going to follow the beaten track and take you the shortest distance between two points, but as far as possible take the most attractive lanes. All of these are well surfaced: Devon is a spider's web of good third-class roads. In the parish of Bradworthy, for instance, a roadman tells me that there are over 50 miles of roads within an area of three square miles. Such roads are narrow and twisting, in some places there is barely room to pass another car without one squeezing into a ditch or making for a gateway. But fortunately they carry little traffic now and are deserted except for the milk lorry and the Post Office van, though it is not safe to drive at more than 30 m.p.h. on these roads. Of course, it is very tempting to any motorist to do as the signposts direct and hurry towards your destination by the shortest possible route. But I assure you, if you do this, the amount of Devon you will see will be negligible and disappointing.

Of all English counties Devon is supposed to be the most beautiful. Indeed its reputation is such that most people have a precise idea of what Devonshire is like even before they go there; and the whitewashed cottages would have to be dazzling and the lanes impossibly steep and narrow to fit in with their preconceptions. But there is no typical Devon scenery. No county has greater variety: nothing could be more dissimilar than the country around Dartmoor to that of Exmoor, nor either of these to the Dart valley and the South Hams; nor is there any similarity between the North Devon coast and what is now little more than the South Devon promenade.

Writing about scenery I feel as though my ink has suddenly turned to treacle. I suspect that is because the whole subject has been so over-written with hack lyricism, more purple than the heather, that it is now difficult to see the country without these associations blurring our vision; this is a pity, for Devonshire has real beauty in it, satisfying without cloying, and interesting without being quaint.

It is difficult to choose which road to take from Exeter. But before leaving this corner of Devon for good, I suggest a drive along the estuary of the Exe taking the side roads and enjoying the scenery across the river. Whatever Exmouth may have been in the seventeenth century, it has now slid into the conformity of a very ordinary seaside resort with little to commend it. By the speed with which Exmouth is growing it is probable that it will soon be joined by a necklace of bungalows to Exeter itself. Driving past these semi-detached conveniences you will wonder why the English are so perverse to spend their time hunting foxes. They would be far better employed hunting architects. Were they to do so, I would not join the Society for the Prevention of Blood Sports. One is justifiably angry at this kind of desecration. Some of the country around here was, until as recently as 1930, as beautiful as any part of the world. It would have been possible to build and not destroy the scenery. But as you will observe, the houses run along the estuary, so that for the most part it cannot be seen any more.

Budleigh Salterton with its bay and lobster pots is a relief after Exmouth and still has some semblance of an identity; after leaving, drive straight to East Budleigh. This is where Sir Walter Raleigh was born.

To my mind, Raleigh is one of the greatest Englishmen of all time. He was what I call a 'whole' man. The range of his talents can be compared

47

to Leonardo's. He is known as a courtier, and as a navigator, but he was very much more than this. He was a considerable poet, and no mean philosopher. He was a great agriculturalist, an inventor, a major statesman (remembering that the word derives from 'estatesman'), and he was also an historian. The very essence of the Elizabethan versatility and range of interest is to be found in this one man, who is a splendid example and prototype.

When you reach East Budleigh you will, after reading the above paragraph, be astounded to find that there is not a single reference to Sir Walter Raleigh in the place. You may wonder whether you have been misled, or whether you have taken the wrong turning, but let me remind you that when I went to Florence because of my admiration for Dante, I could find practically no reference to him there apart from a couple of busts, and the name of the street where I stayed. Certainly I found it impossible to obtain a copy of the *De Vulgari Eloquentia* or the *De Monarchia*, and when I ordered these was asked by the bookseller who had written them. So do not think East Budleigh is the only centre of philistinism. It is not that we have no gods, but very tawdry ones.

Nevertheless you will, if you ask your directions, find your way eventually to Hayes Barton which is about two miles from the village. This is the remarkable Elizabethan manor house where Sir Walter Raleigh was born. It is a perfect example of an Elizabethan manor house, and is unspoilt and in perfect condition. The walled garden in front of the house with the mill-leat and millstone, the farmyard and stables, are probably almost intact and as Raleigh knew them. No wonder he tried to buy his home back again. One wonders how he ever found the resolution to leave it. He born in this house in 1552.

Raleigh spent most of his life trying to persuade a Mr Duke, who had bought Hayes Barton to add to his large estate, to sell it back to him. A letter exists which Raleigh wrote from the Court on 26 July 1584. 'I am most willing to give you whatsoever in your conscience you shall deem it worth because of the natural disposition I have to that place; being born in that house I had rather sit myself there than anywhere else. . . .' In spite of this unconditional offer, Duke refused to negotiate.

Three hundred years later, a rich American tried to move Hayes Barton lock, stock and barrel to Virginia, but was happily frustrated because the walls were of cob, and one beam, 80 feet long, ran the length of the entire house.

Most people know little about Raleigh's writings except, perhaps, the lines he scratched on the glass window of the Queen's chamber:

Fain would I climb yet fear I to fall.

and Her Majesty's reply, scribbled underneath it:

If thy heart fails thee, climb not at all.

But over 20 authentic poems of his exist, and were collected in 1891, published by George Bell and edited by J. Hannah. From references of the period we know that the vast body of his poetic work had been lost. I suspect that some has been appropriated by other names, and a good deal more could be found if sufficient research was done. Only the last book of the poem *Cynthia* exists. There were 20 other sequences. Raleigh's reply to Marlowe's poem *Come live with me and be my love*, which starts '*If all the world and Love were young*' is also worth looking at, as is his *Pilgrimage* which he wrote less than 12 hours before he was beheaded. The quality of the mind that could write:

That, since my flesh must die so soon,
And want a head to dine next noon

just before being beheaded was that of no mere courtier. It may be that the Virgin Queen was his mistress, until he offended her rapacity by wishing to marry one of her ladies-in-waiting. Whereupon she put him in the Tower: and yet Raleigh died wearing the emerald ring she had given him. Though Elizabeth treated him shabbily, as she did others, that he was not too bitter was shown by his immortal description of her:

A lady whom Time hath surprised.

But as I have said, Raleigh was a rounded man, not merely a good poet capable of writing in clear and uncluttered language. He was also an agriculturalist and statesman of the first order. His work in Ireland and his efforts to turn bog into a cultivated estate deserves a volume to itself. And his exploration of New Guinea, the splendid history that he wrote of it and the way that he foresaw that England should look to the West instead of the East, marks him as one of the greatest of the Elizabethans. The history of the world, which he composed for the Prince of Wales while in the Tower of London, indicates the range of his learning, and his ability to write prose. While in the Tower he planned to found a University in London, and what he called 'Queen Elizabeth's Academy for training in the Arts of Navigation, Ship Building, Engineering and the Making of Maps and Charts'. These had been schemes that he had nurtured and had pressed the Court to start throughout his life.

It is strange that a man who lived as well as Raleigh had, in spite of 13 years in the Tower, should have been given an opportunity to make his death even more remarkable. His own defence at his trial, when he came up against men of the calibre of Francis Bacon and Coke, stands out as one of the best ever given in an English Court, not only for its logic, but for the dignity and restraint of his demeanour while making it. In spite of his innocence, though, it availed him nothing: he was condemned; perhaps a man of such outstanding talents as Raleigh could not expect to meet with any other end but the block.

Before his execution, Raleigh asked the headsman to let him feel the edge of the axe, to see if it was sharp.

'I pray thee, let me see it', he said, and felt along the edge. 'This is a sharp medicine but it is a physician for all diseases.' The executioner knelt and begged to be forgiven, and Raleigh placed his hands on his shoulders.

'When I stretch forth my hands, despatch me.' He refused to be blindfolded. 'Think you I fear the shadow of the axe, when I fear not the axe itself?'

He lowered his head on the block and the Dean in attendance asked him if he should not face the east instead of the west, ready for the Lord's rising. 'So that the heart be right, it is no matter which way the head lieth,' Raleigh remarked. He then gave the executioner a signal to raise the axe, but the man could not do so. Raleigh gave him a moment to recover, then signalled again. The crowd became restive, and heard Raleigh's firm voice calling out 'What do you fear? Strike, man, strike!'

The end of this great Elizabethan was witnessed by an unknown poet:

Great Heart! who taught thee so to die?
Death yielding thee the Victory!
Where took'st thou leave of life? If here,
How could'st thou be so far from Fear?
But sure thou died'st and quit'd'st the state
Of Flesh and Blood before that Fate.
Else what a Miracle were wrought,
To triumph both in Flesh and Thought!
I saw in every Stander-by
Pale Death; Life only in thine Eye.
Farewell! Truth shall this Story say,
We died; Thou only lived'st that Day.

I doubt if you will be able to find a copy of Raleigh's poems outside the London Library, but I urge you to read one of the biographies of him and recommend *That Great Lucifer* by Margaret Irwin.

I hope what I have written about the poet will persuade you to go and look at Hayes Barton. It is a splendid house; a rare example of where the best came out of the best.

From East Budleigh I suggest you drive on to Otterton, with its little river running down the main street, reminiscent of Trumpington Street at Cambridge.

The narrow lanes now lead in the direction of Sidmouth. Drive slowly so that you can enjoy the view above the town, and when you enter it don't forget to fill up your picnic basket, by going to the shop at the corner of the High Street, opposite MacFisheries, where they sell a cream cheese which I commend: they also sell Devonshire cream and at least a dozen kinds of local honey.

From Sidmouth you can go, still avoiding the main road, to Branscombe's wooded valley, and stop for a few moments at the Norman church of St Winifred's which has a door of that period. About 50 yards down the valley on the other side of the road there is a building which I found even more interesting than the church, a blacksmith's forge built in 1580, and still worked with a pair of hand bellows. It is fascinating to prod around the shop while the smith bangs away on his anvil. The Inn, 'Ye Old Mason's Arms', further down the road, is worth looking at. As the road leads down such a beautiful valley you may be tempted to go down to the beach, but be warned. I did this and the first thing I observed was a notice which read *Transistor Radios for Hire*. I fled to the next village, Beer.

The fishing village of Beer, a mile from Seaton, was founded by the survivors of a wrecked Spanish boat from the Armada and was known as a site for smugglers in the last century. This precarious and tax-free trade deteriorated with the invention of the telephone which summoned the coastguards. The prosperity of the town has suffered considerably ever since honesty has been imposed upon it.

Sidmouth used to be a very fashionable watering place. In the early nineteenth century members of the Russian royal family came to enjoy its climate: the Romanovs must have been very rigorous.

If you look very carefully in the churchyard at Ottery St Mary you will discover a small, tarnished plaque which states that Samuel Taylor Coleridge was born there. Unlike Raleigh, Coleridge's literary reputation is well established, though to my mind less deserved. Coleridge's father was vicar here, and the poet's childhood was spent in the town. The family was connected with this part of Devonshire for centuries. Several contemporaries reported that Coleridge always spoke with a Devon drawl, but he was more attached to his home town than Ottery St Mary is attached to him. One would have thought that the author of the *Ancient Mariner*, *Christabel* and *Kubla Khan*, not to mention the *Biographia Literaria*, might be someone whom the town would celebrate. But this is not the case.

It angers me to see how great men are ignored, for are there so many of them? I make no apology about dwelling on this fact so often in these pages. Great men are part of the scenery. It is certainly more rewarding to contemplate figures like Raleigh, Gay or Coleridge than to sit admiring the chintzy quaintness of Clovelly High Street. But do not misunderstand me. I am not suggesting that East Budleigh, Barnstaple and Ottery St Mary should sink to the commercialism of Stratford and cash in with cashmere scarves and ashtrays printed with their poets' verses. This is not the kind of live interest in our inheritance that I wish to see. But I am complaining that you cannot buy a single copy of the poems of John Gay in Barnstaple, nor can you find a volume of Coleridge in Ottery St Mary. Indeed, there is no bookshop.

It is possible that our age of mass literacy is going astray somewhere, or has already gone?

From Ottery take the by-road to Clyst Hydon and Westcott and then cross the river Culm on the road to Cullompton and its church.

Cullompton is a very old market town which grew up as a centre for the wool trade. It had a reputation for serge, but there is now no sign of any woollen industry in this district. It arose when the looms were driven by water power and proximity to a river was important. The Devonshire woollen industry collapsed with the invention of steam-machines, after which it moved to the coalfields.

I wish to lead you now to Tiverton: but ignore the signpost which will take you on the main road via Tiverton Junction station. Instead take the narrow lanes across to the village of Ash Thomas; you will probably lose your way, but so much the better, for this is the way to see Devon. You may, looking for Ash Thomas, stumble on Colebrook or Butterleigh or some village neither I nor anybody else has ever discovered.

Tiverton, too, is a very old town with a history reaching back to King Alfred. During the Middle Ages the town flourished under the patronage of the Courtenays, the Earls of Devon, and there is an interesting inscription on one of the Earls' tombs in Tiverton Church.

> *Hoe hoe, who lyes here:*
> *'Tis I, the goode Erle of Devonshere.*
> *With Kate my wyfe, to mee full dere;*
> *That wee spent wee hadde.*
> *That wee gave wee have.*
> *That wee lefte wee loste!*

Tiverton was a wool town too, and the site of serious riots in the last century when the workmen rose up against the use of machinery. Lace was also manufactured here but the town now depends mainly on the farming around it. Once again we have a town with a very ancient history but with very little, apart from the Parish Church, to throw any light on it. The reason for this is that like many other towns in Devon Tiverton has frequently been destroyed by fire. In

1598, 400 houses and 33 persons were destroyed in one outbreak. In 1612, 600 houses were burned leaving little but the castle and the church standing. Apparently the prosperity of the town was such that some were rebuilt, for in 1661 a fire occurred again as it did in 1730, 1762 and 1788. The cause of these fires was thatch.

From Tiverton take the Cadleigh Road, then feel your way to Cadbury and Cheriton Fitzpaine. Having achieved this, finding Stockleigh Pomeroy should present no difficulty to you. After which you can sail direct to Crediton.

I take you to Crediton for one reason alone: it has one of the most beautiful buildings in it in the whole of the West Country. This is the Collegiate Church of the Holy Cross (see illustration). This Norman church was built on the site of the original Saxon Cathedral which stood there when Crediton was the seat of the See of Devon and Cornwall which, under Leofric, was transferred to Exeter. But I will not confuse you with the complicated history of this ancient Saxon town which grew up as a famous centre of the woollen industry. And indeed, apart from the church, little of the original town remains since it was twice destroyed by fire within 20 years, in the eighteenth century. Fortunately, the church remained unscathed.

By the fourteenth century the Norman church had fallen into such disrepair that it had to be rebuilt, and the church which we see today arose. In the eighteenth century it fell into neglect again and the fine medieval ceiling collapsed, being substantially restored in the following century.

Before you enter this perfectly proportioned building you will notice the attractive rose colour of the stone which seems so appropriate to an area where the fields themselves are of rich red loam. The inside of this beautiful church was once decorated in vermilion and gold; traces of the original design can be seen on the south side of the Chancel. The upper part of the font is late Norman. Pieces of early English work, a piscina and holy water stoup, can be seen in the south porch.

Crediton claims to be the birthplace of St Boniface. After he was ordained, Boniface went to Germany and converted the heathen to Christianity until in his 75th year he was 'by faithless Fusians slain'.

I shall be surprised if you do not find this church at Crediton worth visiting.

St Boniface was born at Crediton in 672; he was educated at a Benedictine monastery at Exeter and, like Abelard, became distinguished as a teacher. At the age of 30 he was ordained, and shortly afterwards became Abbot of his monastery. He was only 44 when he left England for the Netherlands, where his missionary work was abortive. He returned to England for a year, then went to Rome where he received the patronage of Pope Gregory II who gave him the name Boniface and sent him as a missionary to Germany. His mission was so successful that he was made Bishop of all Germany east of the Rhine. Germany was, of course, entirely pagan at this period, as it is now. Boniface's first act was to fell Thor's Sacred Oak in the presence of angry tribesmen and priests. He began his work baptising new converts and founding monasteries.

Gregory III appointed him an Archbishop and gave him the task of reorganising the Church in Bavaria and Allemania. In 740 he was re-forming the Frankish Church, having effected a similar achievement in Hesse.

St Boniface was one of the architects of Christendom. It was he who joined the Frankish crown with the Papacy, enabling Charlemagne 30 years later to construct the Holy Roman Empire. Few men had a greater influence on early Europe than this man from Crediton.

After this circular tour across the rivers Exe, Ottery and Culm you will probably be anxious to see nothing but the 'Clarence Hotel' back in Exeter. From Crediton, there is, of course, a main road back to Exeter, and if you take it you will be able to admire the designs of British lorries. Instead, bear with me for a few more bent miles and swing right on the way out of Crediton and thread your way to Tedburn St Mary. I want to persuade you to go to these little villages and hamlets not because any one in particular has any historic monument or is famous for being the birthplace of anybody, but because they are so unpretentious, unspoiled, and unself-conscious. I wonder how many cottages you have fallen in love with? If you have kept to my erratic course you must have admired many.

At Tedburn St Mary you will again be tempted by a bold sign

announcing a road to Exeter. It is the main road from Okehampton. Leave it for those who like going places fast and getting nowhere quickly. And instead of following them turn off to Holcombe Burnet and Ide. This will bring you safely back to your hotel and you will have travelled no more than 100 miles though I admit it may seem a little more judging by the amount you will have seen.

The next day you must be even more resolute for I want you to go to Honiton and Axminster in order to see something of East Devon. But do not touch the A30 which is the main road to Honiton, via Exeter Airport: ignore all the directions which would sweep you on to the Exeter bypass and then flush you along the arterial sewers towards your destination; creep through the city streets up to Pinhoe and then to Dog Village, then on to Whimple, Fenny Bridge, Feniton and Buckerell. Do not try to hurry, for you cannot: these lanes were made for carts. Stop occasionally, and look across towards the Black Down Hills and if you like, curse me a little for leading you astray again. But Honiton is only a couple of miles away.

Before you become too lyrical about the thatched houses you see, you should realise that thatch is the reason why so little remains of the ancient history of these Devon towns. Honiton is a fair example. In 1765 most of the town, including the old chapel of All Hallows, was destroyed by fire, and for this reason nothing remains of the chapel associated with Thomas Becket. Nowadays the town is known for its lace, but as with Axminster carpets very little is in fact manufactured there. The art was brought to the town by Flemish refugees and Shakespeare alludes to it in *Twelfth Night*:

> *The spinsters and the knitters in the sun,*
> *And the free maids that weave their thread with bones,*
> *Do use to chant it.*

From Honiton, take the Lyme Regis road to Axminster. I am tempted to proceed right on to Lyme Regis, a delightful place, but being in Dorset it is out of my present orbit. And you have more than enough to see in Devon.

Axminster is the principal town of East Devon. It is a very ancient town but few signs of its history remain. It is first mentioned as the burial place of Cyneheard in 785. The town grew up in the Middle Ages around the Abbey of Newenham which was founded in 1246, but the magnificent buildings of the Abbey were destroyed. The only other antiquity in the town now is the church which has a fine Norman doorway and there are also examples of medieval tombs.

The town, of course, is known for its carpets but in fact many of these which bear the town's name are now manufactured elsewhere.

The most interesting building in the district is the old farmhouse of Ashe a couple of miles out on the Seaton road. This house is associated with the Drakes and also with another English worthy, being the birthplace in June 1650 of John Churchill, afterwards Duke of Marlborough. In other words, Devon could lay claim to the Churchill family if it wanted to do so.

If we are to keep to your schedule your third day must get you from Exeter to Exmoor. This could be done rapidly by taking the Tiverton road and then going on to Dulverton and Exford. The journey would only take you an hour and a half. But you have already been to Tiverton and I do not want you to double any of your tracks or travel on 'A' or 'B' roads where they can be avoided—and in Devon there is always an alternative route. There are in fact more roads in Devonshire than there are in the whole of Spain. So, this time, I suggest you leave Exeter on the Tiverton road but leave it just after it crosses the river Exe and goes through Bramford Speke. Then follow the river up to Thorverton. From here you will have to cross the tracks you made two days ago at Cadbury, but you can get on to new territory again after a mile or two by driving to Cadleigh Way village and Poughill (not to be confused with the village of the same name which is outside Bude). From Poughill go up to Cruwys Morchard and then cross the main Tiverton–South Molton road and head north to Templeton and Stoodleigh Beacon. This will take you through beautiful wooded country. I am not frightened that my publishing this route will bring about the district's downfall: the lanes are fortunately too narrow for buses and ordinary motorists would lack patience or perseverance to follow it, and besides that, it is landlocked.

From Stoodleigh Beacon go across to Oakford and then join the river Exe again and go to Exebridge and Dulverton. I want you to go to Dulverton because it is the site of the Exe River Fisheries and the trout farm there is well worth a visit, especially if you can persuade the owner to let you see into his hatchery sheds, or watch the big fish being fed in the ponds. Dulverton is on the edge of Exmoor. The best of Devon lies before you—take the Exford road.

THREE

Exmoor

There are three moors in the peninsula, Dartmoor, Exmoor and Bodmin Moor. Of these, Exmoor is easily the most beautiful. I am well aware that not all of Exmoor lies within the boundaries of Devon and that some of it can be claimed by Somerset but I will not be bothered by such trivial and arbitrary geographical details. You will not have known when you have wandered into the terrain of Somerset and I will not prevent you from doing so. At any rate, Exmoor has existed long before these shire boundaries, and it constitutes a geographical entity.

Exmoor is unique. There is no other part of England remotely like it. It is entirely different from Dartmoor, and, I think, has superior scenery. I like the Dorset Downs: I enjoy the wooded park country in Somerset. No doubt the Lake District has its own particular charm and quality, but for all that, Exmoor contains the most beautiful scenery in England. What is so remarkable is that hardly any of it has been spoilt by improvements or ruined by so-called 'public amenities'. Happily there is hardly a garage, public lavatory or even a litter basket on the entire moor.

It must be one of the few remaining tracts of the British Isles where you can look at land without having to see humanity. Dartmoor is also sparsely populated, but its granite outcrop has a depressing poverty about it from which Exmoor is free. Exmoor gives you the essence of country without the sense that it is barren, or abandoned. The country is broken by innumerable undulating valleys threaded by pretty streams. You will be captivated by Exmoor. There is nothing like it in the whole of Europe: I believe parts of California resembled it 50 years ago.

On the maps Exmoor is referred to as a forest. This may mislead you: there are few trees there. Dartmoor is also referred to in old documents as a forest. It means a free range rather than wooded country. There is very little similarity between these two moors. As I say, Exmoor has none of Dartmoor's grim lunar appearance; it does not remind you of prehistory. It is not cruel or desolate. The reason for this difference is, I think, almost wholly due to the fact that Exmoor lacks the outcrops of granite which you see on Dartmoor. The land is well covered and, as the old plough marks show, in places is fairly fertile. There are not stone walls but the lanes are bordered by hedges of beech which are kept clipped. It is one of the few places in England where wild deer still roam. The scenery on the moor is so good that it does not matter from which direction you approach it.

They say that the moor will not exist within a generation, because the plough is nibbling it away, and replaces the heather by grass. Only the other day I saw that Imperial Chemical Industries had taken over a tract of an outlying farm there to experiment with a new herbicide, which may very well make the seeding out of heather land possible without recourse to the plough at all. But even if this cultivation occurs, I do not think more than a marginal area will be threatened, because parts of the moor are still bog-land; it would not be economic to drain them.

If you have followed my suggested route, you will have driven from Dulverton to Exford via Withypool. Exford is a centre of Exmoor hunting. Then take the road to Porlock, turning off at Crooked Post to Luccombe valley. It is no exaggeration to say that this valley with its stream running through it and the wooded hills each side is probably the most beautiful in England. Fortunately most of this area is Trust property, unspoilt and likely to remain so. Luccombe is one of the few areas left in the country which has any walnut trees. It is possible to drive through here in the autumn and collect the nuts from the road. How this timber has escaped the saw-mill with its increasing appetite for furniture is a mystery: and some beneficent hand is still planting walnut saplings to replace any of the old trees. From Luccombe you should take the little road to Oare and go through the Doone Valley down to Simonsbath and Brayford. This is some of the best riding country in England.

Many of these Exmoor valleys still run with herds of wild ponies which, strangely enough, have Arab blood in their veins. Early in the nineteenth century a Mr Knight leased the moors from Sir Thomas Dyke Acland and started a stud with seven or eight Dongola Arab mares, whose descendants are these small wild ponies. He also introduced Cheviot sheep and red deer, and built an enormous mansion which, until it was dismantled, was known as Knight's Folly. It appears Knight was also interested in the moor for its mining possibilities. But in spite of introducing Scotch shepherds and Cornish miners, all his enterprises eventually failed.

The annual fair held at Bampton is the oldest in the West Country. It is the nearest approach England gets to a horse show in the Wild West manner: for on the morning of the fair the wild ponies are rounded up into corrals where the bewildered, shaggy beasts come under the auctioneer's hammer.

Ever since *Lorna Doone* was published in 1869, Exmoor has been known as the Doone country. For years I thought this was an interesting example of where an author's tale had, by being identified with a particular place, created a legend. Generally the reverse process obtains, and the legend gives rise to the story. But in this case I find there is considerable evidence to suggest that Blackmoor did base his story on fact.

It was obviously true that the moors had always been the favourite haunt of outlaws, and some of the more notorious hunting parsons and ruffianly squires lived there. But in 1901 a lady calling herself Ida M. Browne or Audrey Doon wrote an article in the *West Somerset Free Press* which shed light on this subject. She claimed to have been of the original Doone family, and stated that Sir Ensor Doone, the robber chief of Blackmore's story, was the twin brother of the Earl of Moray, who was banished from Doune Castle near Stirling in Perthshire as a result of a family feud. After vainly seeking redress in London, he decided to abandon land and fortune, and turning his face to the setting sun journeyed 13 days westwards with his wife and one servant, until he reached a ruined farmhouse in the East Lyn valley, not far from Oare Ford, and decided to settle there. Miss Doon, in her article, quoted from a diary kept by a member of the family in the eighteenth century which contained the following entries:

> 1747 Sept. 3rd. Went to Barum on my way to the place they call Oare, whence our people came after their cruel treatment by the Earl Moray.
>
> Sept. 7th. Got to Oare and then to the valley of the Lyn. The scenery very bonny like our own land, but the part extremely wild and lonely. Wandered about and thought of the old days of the family there, which I gathered were not peaceable.

Whatever the truth of this is, the ravages of the Doones and the exploits of the highwayman Tom Faggus still colour the moors. An old rhyme runs:

> *Child, if they ask who killed thee,*
> *Say, 'twas the Doones of Badgery.*

Personally I see no reason at all to doubt the existence of such a band, for the isolated country with its half-fortress farmhouses indicates that there was need for protection. I wonder how long Exmoor could remain without village constables before the Doones reappeared—I think it would be only a matter of months.

But quite apart from *Lorna Doone*, Exmoor has produced other works of considerable literary interest. Indeed I think that the two dialect plays, *The Exmoor Scolding* and *The Exmoor Courtship*, are much more interesting than the novel, in that they are genuine products of Exmoor itself. They are almost the only examples of Devon folk-literature.

Of course, one of the attractions about Exmoor is that, unlike Dartmoor and Bodmin, it runs along the coast; you must go over Slattenslade down to Woody Bay and the Valley of the Rocks, where the seascape enhances the moor. You may wonder if the Valley of the Rocks was once peopled by medieval giants, who built castles on every hilltop. But the ruins you see there were never built though what you see looks to be stone placed on top of stone. It is the effect of several million years of soil erosion, no doubt because there are no tree roots to hold the soil in place.

On another trip I suggest you start at the 'Doone Hotel' at Malms-
mead, from which the famous Doone Valley runs. This is the point I
chose for the start of the Golden Horse Shoe Ride, which has a 50-mile
course. Twenty miles of the ride is across Exmoor, through Doone
Valley to Badgworthy Cottage, then along Hockcombe Coombe to
Brendon Two Gates; across Cannonball Down to Exhay and across to
Driver Cottages, and down between Little Vintcombe and Smolla-
combe, past the ruin of Mount Pleasant to Sheracombe Cross, to the
'Poltimore Arms Inn'.

Perhaps you could abandon your car and hire a horse? The motor-car
can only keep to the road, even if it is a Landrover. If you do hire a
horse, then you must also remember to take two Ordnance Survey
maps of the National Grid, Numbers Sheet SS.73 and 74. Without
these you will certainly get lost on the moor, and even with these
you will need a local guide, especially between Badgworthy Cottage
and Brendon Two Gates. Otherwise you will end in a bog, from which
neither you nor your mount will probably ever emerge. But the local
stag-hunts cross this country regularly, and one of them could show
you the way over. If I can persuade you to do this, I think you will
enjoy the ride more than any other part of your visit to the West
Country.

And if you have time drive from Blackmoor Gate via Brayford and
North Heasley to the two Moltons. This road takes you through some
well-timbered country where good forestry is practised.

Arlington Court, the home of the Chichesters, is one of the few
stately homes on Exmoor. It is now the property of the National Trust,
and worth a visit more for the contents of the house than for the
building itself. The original Tudor manor was pulled down. The present
building was designed by a local Barnstaple architect, who had been
an apprentice to Sir John Soane, and the building shows his influence.
The most conspicuous feature of the exterior of the house is the semi-
circular Doric porch. The interior of the house displays many of the
possessions of the Chichesters, who were collectors of pewter and
porcelain. The Sèvres is of particular interest. The outstanding item
in the house is an original water-colour by William Blake depicting

the 'Cycle of The Life of Man'. This picture was discovered only a few years ago on the top of a cupboard in one of the maids' bedrooms. A collection of dresses worn by the family in the latter part of the nineteenth century is displayed on the staircase. It is a pity that the National Trust, by putting so much on view, have reduced the interior of the house to a museum. It is probable that the public would like to see such properties as the homes they were before they fell into the tax collector's maw.

North Molton is not without charm and is known because gold used to be mined there. There are several other indications of minerals in North Devon, including the silver at Combe Martin and the seam of coal at Hartland.

But South Molton is a town of considerable architectural distinction, though quite unaware of its Georgian and Regency houses. One of the best Regency houses in Devonshire is there, facing the square, now used as a chemist's shop.

It was here at South Molton that Charles II was first proclaimed King of England, when there was the abortive uprising under Penruddock in 1655. The leaders of this rebellion were taken to Exeter, tried and executed. Most of the Devonians who had sustained them were shipped as slaves to the tobacco plantations in Virginia, which may account for the second injection of Devonian blood into America, and the large number of Devonian phrases and terms which are still current Yankee idiom.

When you come to leave Exmoor, I suggest you take the coast road to Barnstaple via Combe Martin.

Combe Martin enjoys an ideal position on the coast where the cliffs have a grandeur which even contemporary architecture cannot besmirch. The town is supposed to have traded with Venetian galleys, but there is no evidence for this. The market was established in 1264 and Combe Martin was then known already for its silver and lead mines. Sir Walter Raleigh was interested in the mining in the district and the City of London still owns a silver cup made from silver mined from Combe Martin weighing 136 ounces. The inscription on it gives evidence of its origin:

Dispersed I in earth did lye
   Since all beginninge olde
In place called Combe, where Martin long
   Had hid mee in his molde.
I dydd no service on the earth,
   And no manne sate mee free,
Till Bulmer by his skill and charge
   Did frame me this to be.

It is said that the ore from the mines in this area yielded between 140 and 150 ounces of silver to the ton.

Ilfracombe looks like a holiday town vomited up by nineteenth-century industrialism, though in fact this is not the case, for it has a long history. The original town was called Aelfricombe and was noted for its harbour in the twelfth century, maintaining an important traffic with Wales and Ireland. At the siege of Calais, when Liverpool only managed to contribute one ship, Ilfracombe was able to send six. Many chapels were established by the missionaries along the coast when they came to North Devon to try to convert the inhabitants to Christianity. Their efforts were apparently unsuccessful. In the fifteenth century the town was a place of pilgrimage. In a sense, it is so today. It is not that we have no gods, but strange gods.

Now take the road (B3343) out to Woolacombe, then drive to Georgeham and walk out to Baggy Point. This is the bit of country which Henry Williamson has made all his own. As a writer he is sadly undervalued today, but his time will come. I have not the critical equipment to comment on his novels, but his writing on nature has been equalled only by Hudson and surpassed by no one. He is part of the Devon scenery.

FOUR

North Devon

One can gauge the importance that Barnstaple once had by the spider's web of roads which still lead to this town on the banks of the Taw. Barnstaple claims to be the capital of North Devon and has been since it was called Barum at the time of the Roman occupation. The town used to be entirely enclosed by walls. No sign of these remain except in the name of Boutport Street which used to circumvent the walls. The bridge is seven centuries old and was constructed by public subscription. The original begging letter asking for donations refers to the river there as a 'great, hugy, mighty, perylous, and dreadfull water, where-as salte water doth ebbe and flowe foure tymes in the day and the night', and offering 'a gentle dirge and masse solemly sung' to all benefactors. The bridge was widened in 1964.

There is some question as to whether Bideford or Barnstaple sent more ships to fight the Armada. Both towns claim the superiority. This lies behind all the rivalry between them. But it was Barnstaple which gave hospitality to Huguenot refugees. The story is that a party landed on the quay one Sunday morning and were standing destitute in the town when the people came out of the Parish Church. One of the parishioners took a couple of refugees home for Sunday dinner and he recommended that other people in the congregation should follow his example. This spontaneous piece of social integration was reached without any hectoring from sociologists or planners. The Huguenots brought Barnstaple a new prosperity. It is still a well-to-do town but only one of its potteries is now working. It was a centre for potting during the Roman occupation.

But undoubtedly Barnstaple's first claim to fame is that the poet John Gay was born and raised here, though the author of *The Beggar's Opera* receives scant respect from the town.

John Gay was born in Joy Street in Barnstaple in 1685. He attended Barnstaple Grammar School, and lived in the town until he went to London in his early twenties. He frequently returned to his home town, and his family lived there for many years.

The only relic of Gay in Barnstaple is his chair, and it is doubtful whether everything is authentic. In the Queen's Hall, which was built in the 1930s, there is a room which bears his name. But that is the only sign of Gay in Barnstaple today. None of his manuscripts is to be seen; no books can be bought; there is no monument, and what is worse, no interest in his work there.

Gay is an important figure of the Augustan Age. He contributed to the *Spectator* and was a colleague of Addison and Steele. Later he became the close friend of Alexander Pope and Jonathan Swift. Gay, Pope and Swift made the Triumvirate of Letters which, in my opinion, represents one of the highest points of English literature. These three poets respected each other, inspired each other, and were seldom, if ever, out of touch, even when Gay was taking the waters at Bath with his inseparable companion, the Duchess of Queensbury. When Pope was hibernating at Twickenham, complaining of his health, and the Dean was being at his most splenetic, writing the famous Drapier Pamphlets from Dublin, the correspondence between these three poets continued; it contains the essence of the eighteenth century. What the Italian Renaissance is to painting, so the Augustan Age is to English literature, and that contribution was made by Pope, Swift and Gay. When these three were staying together at Twickenham, Pope was writing the *Dunciad*, Swift was finishing *Gulliver's Travels*, and Gay had his *Fables* in his pocket and was writing *The Beggar's Opera*. Pope and Swift recognised Gay's genius: Barnstaple did not and does not. One would think that in an age which is so obsessed with education as this one is, that the town had every excuse to build a theatre in the poet's memory in which to give performances of *Polly* and *The Beggar's Opera* at least once a year. You may have seen Brecht's *Threepenny Opera* and enjoyed it. I think it is a masterpiece, largely because of Kurt Weill's

8 Bridge across the River Taw, Barnstaple

music. The book itself is largely derivative from Gay. Sometime, perhaps, you will have the opportunity of seeing Gay's original *Beggar's Opera*. Benjamin Britten made an excellent realisation of it. It is a work which can never fail to find its place in a repertoire. *Polly* proved less popular when it was originally presented; indeed, it was banned: it should be revived.

Gay also wrote the libretto for Handel's *Acis and Galatea*. He died in 1732 and was buried in Westminster Abbey. The lines on his tomb:

> *Life is a jest, and all things show it;*
> *I thought so once, and now I know it*

were written, of course, by Gay himself.

St Brannock's Church at Braunton is one of the few parish churches in Devonshire to have escaped the destructive hand of the Puritans. None of the original church built on this site in the ninth century remains. The leaden-slated spire is similar to the parish churches at Barnstaple (1389) and Torrington. The present building is thirteenth-century, and the internal furnishings are of a later date. Again we see the barrel-shaped roof, carved chestnut pews, and a nave without equal in the whole county. The pews, too, are of particular interest. Each has two carved ends, and no design is repeated. The benches themselves are adze-hewn, about four inches thick. Each part of the pew consists of a single piece of timber. They date from between 1500 and 1600. The Braunton pews are similar to those at Morthoe, High Bickington, Atherington and Lapford. Many of the bench ends are carvings of initials, presumably of the people who originally occupied them. It will be noticed that some of these initials are inverted, or carved the wrong way round. The only explanation for this is a local tradition to the effect that the inverted initials were to signify the humility of the donor of the pew.

The pews, however, are not the only fine pieces of woodwork to be found in the church. There are some excellent Jacobean works in the organ loft and pulpit. The present altar rails appear to be a Georgian addition of rather crude workmanship. There are three thirteenth-century lancet windows on the north side.

9 The River Torridge at Bideford

Also in the Lady Chapel of the church is a fine Portuguese dower chest, which is supposed to be a relic from the Armada.

Braunton contains some quaint tombstones in the churchyard. Against the south wall of the Lady Chapel is a stone to the memory of Mistress Deborah Keene:

> Here lyeth interred Mrs Deborah Keene, late
> owner of the manor of Braunton Arundel in this parish.
> She was baptized Feb. 24, 1627, lived
> unmarried, and was buried Dec. 31, 1694.
>   Virginity was held in estimation,
> And wont to be observed with veneration.
> Above 'tis still so—single life is led;
> In heaven none marry, nor are married
> But live angelic lives, and virtuous around
> All with their coronets the Lamb surround.
>   This maiden lady has one obtained,
> Who though much sought in marriage still refrained
> And now the inheritance undefil'd obtained.

Another lettered tombstone states:

> Thomas—May 27, 1833. 23 years.
> His death was Sudden and unexpected
> Being Occasioned by a fall from
> A ROCK, Which, instantly, removed
> Him from Time to Eternity.
> Here unto all you standers
> By: as you am now, So once was
> we; as we am now: so you mus be,
> Prepare for death and follow we.

And as at Penfold Parish Church, there is at the bottom of the grave-yard a Guild House which was clearly constructed to house the masons who were employed to build the church. It is in a fine state of preservation with carvings on the beams over the door, and two original Elizabethan windows, overlooking the archway. Part of this Guild House is now used for the manufacture of poultry-food; it should be an ancient monument.

When I think of Devon, I find that I do not visualise either Dartmoor or Exmoor, or even the cliffs that I have known so long. I think of the rivers; Taw, Torridge, Tamar and Teign. The best of scenery is always where there is a river. I think rivers are the most graceful things in nature. They seem to lend the country through which they flow a vitality engendered from their own movement, and a serenity reflected from their quiet pools. A river suggests affluence and assures fertility. The country seems contained by its course: and although in fact it is the land which determines the river's direction, I always get the impression that the river is unrestricted and flows only where it can protect the land most.

A river is the very antithesis of a moor. On Dartmoor one cannot escape the feeling of the essential inhumanity, of being out of one's element. It is just as if one was at sea. It is in a valley through which a river flows that human values seem most important. While on a moor, we are faced with the indifference of nature towards all that we believe—however foolishly; and then we turn from the bleak winds of its essential nihilism to the sheltered valley from which all humanity is derived.

And if a river has no other justification than that it is something which the Devonians have had to bridge, it is enough. My taste in architecture may be perverse, but I think that the large bridge at Bideford across the Torridge, the fine Brunel bridge at Saltash and the small one-coach toll bridges over the Avon and the Dart, are not only the best buildings in Devon, but by being well built are the most beautiful. The width of the river has imposed the throw of the bridge. The strength of the flow has determined the solidity of the piers. When we build to a form so precisely defined, we escape those extraneous exuberances which mar so many of our churches, for example.

I think that if you want to see the best scenery of Devon and pass through some its prettiest towns, you should abandon the roads altogether and take a small boat up any one of its rivers.

The Torridge, from the estuary mouth at Westward Ho! to where it rises near Bradworthy, covers as great a variety of scenery as can be found over the entire county. By the estuary, the country is a mixture of low-lying pasture, mudflats and sand dunes; the latter were some of the finest preserves in the country for wild birds until the War Office took them over. The flatness of the country here reminds one more of Norfolk than the West Country, though only a few miles off lie the headlands of Clovelly and Bucks Mills.

A mile or two up the river is Appledore, so genuine a fishing village that it almost topples into the little boats, which are beached underneath the houses. Seen from the river the village is a clutter of cottages, with the washing and nets filling the back yards, and the sprawl of children scrabbling over derelict hulks on the rocks below. But walking along the narrow main street, one is struck by the nautical tidiness of these same houses, the trim doors with their polished brasses. It is a village which was certainly never planned, and one suspects never built, but just grew, as things do grow in Appledore.

Appledore is one of the few remaining villages where wooden boats are still made, mostly from oak heartwood, with their joints fitted so nicely that they are watertight. The timber is still shaped with the adze, and tree-nails are used instead of metal bolts. Sails and fishermen's jerseys are also made there, and an Appledore man can be recognised anywhere by his jersey: at least two pounds of wool go into each one.

Instow and Fremington, across the river, have nothing like the same character, but they do keep up a tradition of yachting and the white sails enliven the scene.

You will be wondering where to stay while touring North Devon. I recommend Bideford. It is not only my home town but my favourite town. I have already suggested that you stay at 'Tanton's Hotel' on the Quay.

Bideford, a few miles up river, plainly grew up around the toll gates at each end of the bridge (see illustration), the foundations of which are reputed to be wool sacks, the only material at that time which would stand firm in the ebb and flow of the current. Even today the Bridge Authority plays a large part in the affairs of the town. Like Appledore it has always been connected with ships, and first rose to be of importance during Queen Elizabeth's reign, when the Bideford fleet took a large part in the cod-fishing off newly-discovered Newfoundland. Up to the end of the nineteenth century there was a large rope-making industry there, and the posts to which hemp was attached for plaiting still stand in Mill Street. It was also very well known for its pottery. And today, Bideford ware are collector's pieces. The Quay-side where ships berth from Sweden, Holland and other countries is at the same time the principal street of the town, with the best shops and offices overlooking the river. I know of no other town in England where you have the advantage of being able to watch the fascinating activity of boats loading and unloading without any of the squalor and dirt which usually go with a dock.

Bideford was the birthplace of Kingsley, the author of *The Water Babies* and *Westward Ho!* Unlike Barnstaple, Bideford has erected a statue to its famous writer. It stands on the Quay. I am unable to recommend Kingsley's works.

Bideford has no particular reputation for its architecture. But it contains some excellent examples of Queen Anne, Georgian and Regency houses. None of them are show-pieces, and Bideford seems unaware of their existence; the ground floor of one of its Regency houses has been turned into a tyre shop.

It is as closely connected with land as with the sea, and its cattle market is one of the principal centres for the North Devon beef breed.

The Torridge Vale runs along the river banks between Bideford and Torrington. I urge you to make this drive. It is a graceful and most fertile valley. About half-way along it you will see Weare Gifford set beside the river. That is, if you will stop the car and look over the stone wall which runs along the road. The village has a peaceful and solid appearance: in some ways its stone reminds one of the Cotswolds. Weare Gifford cannot claim any place in history. It is quite content to sit embraced by the river Torridge and is known only for its strawberry-beds.

Torrington, at the end of the valley, stands pretentiously on the top of its hill. It has Roman foundations, but they are not visible: what is apparent is a disappointing main road bordered by semi-detached cot-tages reminiscent of a mining village in Scotland, though the village square has a more pleasing appearance. The 'Black Horse Inn' here was where General Fairfax received the final capitulation of the Royalist forces. Something from the sorrow of that occasion still seems to brood over this tavern.

The Parish Church of St Michael at Torrington was rebuilt in 1651, the original church having been blown up by 80 barrels of gunpowder in 1645. Cromwell's cavalry used Salisbury Cathedral as a stable, and it is not surprising to discover that they used the original St Michael's church as an arsenal. Some of the fourteenth-century stonework survived the explosion, including the bosses of the tower, and the north transept. A small amount of stone carving on the north-eastern arcade is also of an earlier period than the restored church.

Torrington church originally had a spire of leaden slates similar to those at Braunton and Barnstaple, also built in the fourteenth century. The explosion destroyed this. A new tower was built, but within a few years it was blown down in a gale and fell through the roof of the church.

Various details on the exterior are worth noting, including the ornamented lead rain-water pipes and fragments of carving of the early thirteenth century which were built into the south wall.

Inside, we see again a wagon-shaped roof with plaster carvings and carved bosses at the intersections, those in the chancel still being gilded and coloured.

Two of the gravestone inscriptions at Torrington are worth noticing. One to John Clark and his wife:

> *Two lie underneath this stone,*
> *Rather the two halves of one.*
> *Two they were, so like, so even*
> *Natured, statured, bred, that Heaven*
> *Made them one by wedlock knot;*
> *Whom e'en death divided not.*

Near the south porch is a stone which bears this inscription;

> *She was*
> *But words are wanting*
> *To say what!*
> *Think what a wife should be*
> *And she was that.*

Another:

> *Here lies a man who was killed by lightening,*
> *He died when his prospects seemed to be brightening;*

He might have cut a flash in this world of trouble,
But the flash cut him, and he lies in the stubble.

There are few houses in Torrington worth noticing, but there is one, No. 28 South Street, which dates from 1701. This has a fine façade and an extremely interesting plaster canopy over the street entrance. Inside there is a unique ceiling in a room on the ground floor which carries mouldings of a dozen or more musical instruments imposed one upon the other to make a central figure.

From Torrington take the side-road to Frithelstock, then on to Bradworthy. I doubt if you will ever emerge from this route; as I have said elsewhere, it is a maze of narrow lanes, most of which, as the signposts show, are leading to Woolfardisworthy. But you will probably never reach this place, nor, if you do, know you are there, because it is also called Woolsery. But, I repeat, there is only one way to see the best of Devonshire if you are motoring, and that is to lose your way. I mean that literally: it is, fortunately, very easy to do. The signposts were for the most part erected by locals who, because they know that 'X' is on the way to 'Y', assume that every traveller should know it or has no right being in the county. Other directions are casual, some are downright perverse or merely misleading. A favourite trick is to erect a post pointing in the direction of some town and then at the next cross-road fail to make any mention of this town again. It is as if the Devonian signposts had been designed to keep you forever motoring round the country.

I remember one signpost in North Devon which stood at a fork of four lanes. Each finger on the post had Woolfardisworthy on it, and yet pointed in opposite directions. As a matter of fact these four lanes did lead by four different routes to this old Saxon hamlet. But many a traveller was known to go berserk at the sight of this post. At the time when we were expecting a Nazi invasion during the last war, all these signposts were hurriedly removed to prevent them being of assistance to enemy parachutists. At the time I pointed out that it would have been far better to leave all the signposts to assure that the enemy never reached anywhere; but my advice was not taken. You may wonder why. But I beg you not to become frustrated and angry by these posts. I want you to lose yourself, and these directions will guarantee that you do. Just accept them as vagaries, as eccentric as the weather, and be surprised if you happen to find yourself where you intended.

Driving around North Devon you are bound to notice the number of ugly chapels in villages too small to support even their own church. What spiritual fervour produced them?

In spite of the fact that Wesleyanism was ill received in Devon in 1743, when John and Charles Wesley made their first tour into the West Country, there are several reasons why it appealed to the population. In the first place the farmers were disgusted at paying heavy tithes to the Church and seeing no return for their money. Secondly, Wesley appealed to the growing liberalism of the people, who were tired of voting with their landlords, who withheld a tenancy if the tenant did not agree with their own political views. Finally, of course, many of the parsons had become much more interested in hunting than in tending their flock. Some of these hunting parsons have become legendary figures: you may have noticed that in many villages the vicarage stables are a large as the vicarage, which itself is bigger than the church.

The two best-known figures were the Rev. Jack Russell of Swimbridge, near Barnstaple, and John Froude, vicar of Knowstone. Jack Russell, it appears, did not neglect his pastoral duties; but there is a story told of him that when interviewing a prospective curate, who failed to follow Russell on horseback over a five-bar gate, he said, 'If you can't leap a five-barred gate like that, I'm sure you can't preach a sermon. Good-bye.'

John Froude's eccentricity was more vicious. He was reputed to keep a gang of toughs in his vicarage, and if one of his parishioners could not pay his tithe, his barn would be burnt down or his horse lamed.

John Boyce, rector of Sherwell, wishing to hunt with Sir Thomas Acland over Exmoor one Sunday, told his clerk to give out a notice. The following appeared on the church door;

> This to give notiss—there be no sarvice to
> this church this arternoon; cos maester be

78

a-going over the moor a stag-hunting wi
Sir Thomas.

My own parish contains another story of this kind. One Sunday, when the snow was lying deep on the ground and the vicar was reading the second lesson, a man opened the church door and shouted 'I've got 'un', whereupon the whole congregation, including the vicar, rose up and followed him, and within a couple of hours had found and dug up a fine old fox from his earth; all then repaired to the village inn.

If it was not hunting, it was, of course, wrecking; and there is a tale that when the Reverend Hawker was preaching one day at Morwenstow, a man came up to him and whispered something in his ear. Hawker motioned him to be silent, and continued with his sermon. As it was drawing to an end, he was seen to take off his surplice in the pulpit. He then went down the aisle and announced; 'Gentlemen, a Dutch ship has just come in under Highcliff; now we all start even', and with that he bolted out of the door, leaving the congregation still on their knees.

How far these tales are typical of Devonshire is not certain, but one can be sure that in the eighteenth century there were many parsons who were mainly concerned with horses and hunting for two obvious reasons: the horse was their only means of transport, and the hunted hare the mainstay of their larders.

Wesleyanism was able to appeal against this 'looseness', and gave an added incentive to its adherents; for the itinerant preachers took orders for seeds and manures, and were, in a way, the first commercial travellers in the West Country.

The present picture is of many rural parsons living in vicarages which were built for a style of living that can no longer be maintained, and of parishes being joined together since they cannot support a parson of their own. And the chapels too are now ill attended. Already several old vicarages have become guest houses, and some chapels turned into youth hostels.

Before you leave Bideford I urge you to take the boat from the Quay (ascertaining sometime before which days of the week it sails) and go over to Lundy.

*11 Clovelly : where a waterfall of cottages
meets the sea*

I have known Lundy Island all my life—I can see it even now from my window as it sits like an upturned pie-dish at the mouth of the Bristol Channel: and I have been across there many times.

It was my first visit which made me grateful to the place. I was in my early twenties and was trying to emerge from a period of unusual dissipation. My mother had suggested that a few days on the island might brace me up. I doubted this; my moral disintegration was deep-seated. However, I flew there, the pilot somehow managed to land in spite of the hazards of herds of wild ponies grazing between the gorse and heather-covered runway. After this shock, I went straight to the Inn; standing at the bar, feeling very unsure of any bearings in this world or any other, the landlord of the pub eventually approached me.

'We wonder, Sir, whether you would be good enough to take a Service in our Church? We haven't had a vicar on the island for a very long time.'

I felt my collar to see whether I had forgotten to put a tie on.

'If you will agree, I will arrange to have the Church bell rung.'

'What makes you think I'm a vicar?' I asked.

'The way you talk and you look like a man of serious moral principles.'

I gulped my brandy, disabused the landlord but thanked him profusely for repairing my morale so effectively. Half an hour later, I was amusing myself with a fruit machine in the bar when all the winter's savings of the islanders seemed to pour at my feet. I was able to stand drinks to the entire population of 13 adults; it was a service that lasted some time. I believe my congregation enjoyed my mission.

Some encyclopaedias are wrong about Lundy; one of them describes the island as '50 miles off the north-west coast of Devon, five miles long and two miles broad'. In fact, Lundy is only 12 miles from the mainland. Its length is three miles and its breadth only half a mile.

It has a very ancient history and it is a question how the island was originally populated. Being almost 19 miles from a convenient crossing point on the Devon coast, the crossing is extremely rough and would certainly defy any coracle. In spite of these facts there are graves on the island which prove that it was inhabited in the Stone Age. One can speculate what kinds of boats the Stone Age dwellers used. It is clear that a people who could cross these 19 miles must have been very much more organised than we have previously thought.

These graves on Lundy are interesting for several reasons. In one huge stone kist skeletons measuring eight feet and more were unearthed. These look like a race of giants, yet we have been told that Stone Age man was very much below our average height. If that is so, the Lundy giants were from a race which is now entirely extinct.

There is no historical reference to Lundy of any kind until the twelfth century, when it was fortified by Jordan de Marisco who had married Agnes, the daughter of Henry II's brother. Marisco's revolt led to his forfeiting the island, which was then granted to the Knights Templars.

The Mariscos regained the island in 1281 only to be dispossessed again in 1321 when it was granted to the King's favourite, Hugh le Despencer. After le Despencer's fall, on the accession of Edward III, the island reverted to the Crown. Eventually, it was conveyed to Sir Richard Grenville, and for a time was held by the Leveson-Gower family.

In James I's reign it was known as a haunt of pirates and was held by Captain Salkeld. It is not known what happened to him, but he must have vacated the island in time for the infamous Judas Stucely to use it as a place of refuge after his betrayal of Sir Walter Raleigh on the Thames, when he handed the great navigator and poet over to the most despicable king in English history. In 1625 the island was occupied by a Turkish squadron and later by Spaniards, though there is some doubt over how long they stayed.

All the same, historians agree that Lundy has always been a graveyard for shipping. Take any year—1856, for instance. In that one year 173 boats were wrecked in the Bristol Channel, and of these 97 were smashed on the east coast of the island, and 76 were lost on the west coast. Nowadays, of course, Trinity House has a lighthouse and foghorn there; but even so, I myself have known of several boats which have been beaten to pieces against Lundy's granite cliffs. As an old poem I found says:

This Lundy is a nymph to idle toys inclined,
And all on Pleasure set, doth wholly give her mind;
A lusty, black-browed girl, with forehead broad and high
That often had bewitched the seagods with her eyes.

'A lusty black-browed girl with forehead broad and high' is rather a romantic description of the sinister cliffs which scowl down at you, and round which the fat puffins fly incessantly, uttering their monotonous and unmelodious cry.

The puffins have something to cry about, for Lundy has suffered so much, and most of this at the hands of the pirates which infested the Bristol Channel and used the island as their base. In the reign of James I a special commission was formed at Barnstaple to inquire into the robberies by pirates from Lundy.

In 1625 the Mayor of Bristol reported that 'three Turkish pirates have surprised and taken the Island of Lundy making the inhabitants their slaves and they have threatened to burn Ilfracombe'. This report was true, for the Turks not only stayed a fortnight on Lundy, but carried away 60 of the inhabitants as prisoners to work on their ships.

Yet the Bristol Admiralty did very little but form Committees of Inquiry. Nobody was sure to which department Lundy belonged, and nobody was keen to have the responsibility. Five years later, in 1630, a Captain Plumleigh reported that 'Egypt was never more infested with caterpillars than the Channel with pirates. Some have attempted to land on Lundy, but the inhabitants hurled boulders down the cliff and happily slaughtered the lot of them'. How they did this I do not know —that is, if the population had really been taken off by the Turks only five years before. The very next year a Spanish man-of-war landed 80 men on the island. And as an old report says: 'They burned our farms, took away our young sheep and our daughters, and left us only old ewes and old women.' It's worth noting that they put the sheep before the women. The islanders then complained to King Charles, but he was too busy with his own pirates to trouble with theirs, and Lundy continued to suffer.

Even in the reign of William and Mary she found no peace, for a ship, pretending to be Dutch, sent a boat ashore desiring some milk for their captain who was sick. They asked permission to land and the unsuspecting islanders granted this request. After a few days, the crew informed the islanders that their captain had died. They begged permission to bury him in the consecrated ground near the church and invited all the islanders to attend the burial service. Fond of a good funeral, they accepted the invitation. But when the corpse was brought into the church they were all asked to go outside for a few minutes, whilst the Dutch said their own prayers over their dead captain. The guileless inhabitants of Lundy stood waiting in the graveyard, only to be surprised by the pirates who, armed with weapons which had been carried in the coffin, rushed out of the church and made them all prisoners. These pirates then took 50 horses, 300 goats, 500 sheep and some bullocks. What they could not take away they threw into the sea. They even stripped the inhabitants of their clothing and then, throwing the guns of Lundy over the cliff, left her once more in a destitute and disconsolate condition.

But the history of Lundy is more colourful than true, and it is worth remembering that the story of the captain in a coffin on Lundy is identical with the legend of how the English captured the island of Sark from the French.

In 1747 a Thomas Benson, one-time Member of Parliament for Barnstaple, entered into a contract for the exportation of convicts to Virginia or Maryland, but it appears that Benson obtained a lease of Lundy Island, and instead of sending the convicts to America, took them to Lundy to put them to work for his own profit. The men probably worked in the granite quarries, and this may explain why Lundy granite was used for the Thames Embankment.

By mentioning Lundy's unhappy history I hope I am not dissuading you from visiting this island. Though the pirates have gone, the island still boasts the greatest variety of sea birds of any place in the British Isles.

Lundy is also interesting from a legal and political point of view. The island has always been privately owned. In the eighteenth century it was sold by auction, with a collection of books bracketed together in the lot, and the whole fetched under £20.

Today, Lundy is owned by a Mr Harman. He is the Lord of Lundy, sole owner, governor and justice. Twenty years ago his father approached me with the idea of opening a casino there, and he told me some interesting facts about his 'vest-pocket dominion', as he called it. Apparently the island, though it is under the British Crown, is still independent in many respects. For instance, the Lundy islanders pay no taxes. There is no tithe there and the Church of England can only land a priest with the owner's consent. The only public house is open when anybody wants a drink—I have never known it closed. And the 12 inhabitants are exempt from all those innumerable restrictions which are our particular kind of freedom on the mainland. Lundy is a feudal state with an autocratic ruler; but that does not seem to worry it. Indeed, as I sit here in Devon hedged in by democratic freedoms and look across to that bastion of baronial privilege I often wonder why the devil I don't become one of Mr Harman's tenants.

Clovelly, on the coast opposite Lundy, is another feudal property: that is to say, it is an old manor entirely owned and ordered by one person. The village has an unmistakable Spanish or Portuguese atmosphere. This may not be accidental; it is quite possible that it was partially built by Spanish sailors cast ashore from wrecks of the Armada. The narrow cobbled path, known as the High Street, which crawls up from the little jetty is similar to many Spanish villages bordering the Mediterranean. It is the only High Street in England so precipitous that donkeys are the only means of transport. Even the postman has his donkey, and all fish caught in the bay have to be hauled up on wooden sleds, which the donkeys then take down again loaded with coal or provisions.

Many of the cottages still boast ships' timbers with which they were originally constructed. The woodcarvings of fruit and flowers decorating some of the front doors are certainly continental.

Seen on a spring morning, with the nets drying on the quay, and the sun shining on the clear colour-washed walls, with the intermittent procession of donkeys being goaded up the path, it is hard to believe one is in England. But as you climb slowly upwards past trim window boxes, with glimpses into even trimmer front parlours, and hear the tourists cooing 'how quaint', as they buy Birmingham brasses to carry back to their charabancs, the illusion is unfortunately somewhat dispelled. The fact that the whole village is kept in good repair and extremely tidy, with not even an advertisement to blemish its appearance, makes it a showplace. Like so many places which enjoy a unique situation, the self-conscious and almost deliberate exploitation of the picturesque partly defeats its own ends. One suspects that the donkeys have been hired for the season: that the old fishermen are too genuine to be true; and the cottages too spruce to be lived in. Perhaps if one stayed till the autumn one would see the donkeys returned to the contractor's field, the men slink off to the nearest industrial suburb to revert to factory hands and the cottages swathed in dust sheets. One expects any moment to step behind the backcloth and find the whole is a film set.

But justifiable as this charge is against many Devon tourist centres, Clovelly is genuine. It is we who are so used to the fake that we sense it even where it does not exist. The place has remained unspoilt architecturally: no bungalows pimple the cliffs, and no enterprising spiv has yet made his fortune there from a fun-fair.

The reason for such restraint lies not in the lack of opportunity, but in the owner's sense of values. Here is an example of private property at its best, of a place being kept in trust for the nation and not by the nation.

Although Devon has a long coastline of approximately 200 miles, very little fish is landed now compared with the days before steam trawling was introduced. The value is little more than a few hundred thousand pounds a year. Plymouth and Brixham are the only two large ports, and most of the fish landed is caught from small fishing villages, such as Budleigh Salterton, Hope Cove, Dartmouth, Clovelly, Ilfracombe, Seaton and Sidmouth. At the Yealm mouth there is an oyster fishery, though it is dependent on brood oysters imported from Brittany.

Trawling and lobster-pot fishing is done by men who for the most part work in small family-owned boats. It is worth while to go out in one of these boats, either from Bideford or Clovelly, to see the net hauled up. As it surfaces, one sees the hideous hermit crabs and fantastic starfishes caught in the opening: but farther down in the sleeve there are a couple of giant rayfish with their great wings and poisonous tails. They haul on, carefully folding the net as they go and shaking off great globular lumps of transparent squid spawn, and then in the final pocket there is the tail of the porpoise still lashing holes into the net. The rest of the catch consists of two dozen plaice, four rayfish, a red gunnet with wings tipped with violet and blue so that it looks like a bizarre ballet-dancer, and finally a dozen dog fish. The latter are eventually skinned and sold as rock salmon. As soon as the catch is emptied on to the deck the net is thrown overboard again and the second and final drag for the day back across the bay begins.

Whilst chugging slowly along the fishermen begin sharpening their knives on a pebble preparatory to cleaning their catch. As soon as they begin, gulls begin to sweep out from the cliffs two miles off, and in a few minutes a whole cloud of them are shrieking and diving for titbits beside the boat. The gulls can see a net taken from the sea from over three miles off. At the end of the day, after 12 hours' dragging, the fishermen might have three boxes in all.

Most Devon fishermen are fishmongers themselves; and each plaice in the box was already promised for a favoured customer. I asked the owner of the boat whether this was an average catch. He considered it was, and put its value at about £3 10s.

Considering the boat was worth £3,000 and making allowances for use of oil, wear and tear of nets, etc., together with two men's work for 12 hours, this catch did not seem very profitable. Yet such men take appalling risks to life and capital every day for a meagre profit of a few shillings. Why do they do so? The answer is probably as complex as the nets they fish with; it is certainly not for gain alone. For it is certain that these fishermen spring from the same stock as the famous Elizabethan sailors: and for centuries they have eked their living from the ocean—with probably a little smuggling to help them over the worst patches.

A Devon fisherman is by nature as optimistic as a gold prospector. If he had a bad catch today, he hopes it will be better tomorrow, and he never hauls his net up without the secret hope that, this time, it will be the talk of the village.

But much could be done to improve the size of the catches. In the first place many of the jetties need repair: harbours could be extended and thus enable the men to go out at high or low tide. They have applied to 'Lunnon' for help, and have pleaded that if this work was done they could treble their catch; but 'Lunnon' won't listen. For after all, it is much more economical for England to import rock salmon from Canada and lobster from California than let Devonians catch it off Devonshire.

Freshwater fishing in Devonshire is also neglected. The best rivers are polluted, lacking fish passes at weirs, and their level has been lowered by the drawing off of water for the use of towns.

The salmon which you see in Devon shops does not come from Scotland. One evening I was driving over a small bridge across the river Torridge when I saw a man gaff a large fish further down the bank and slip it under his raincoat. The methods of poachers have always intrigued me, so two evenings later I walked down the towpath of the river, which is more than 20 feet wide at this point.

Suddenly, about 50 yards ahead I saw someone leap back from the edge of the river, pick up a sack and run off as fast as he could. Meanwhile I saw three other men on the opposite bank, who took but a mild interest in the affair, and were sauntering off among the willows. The man ahead of me still ran as hard as he could go.

Obviously he took me for a water bailiff. I decided to frighten him by giving chase. When he saw I was following him he turned and scrambled through a hedge and away over a ploughed field, still dragging his sack. For a quarter of a mile I pursued, until I was at the point of complete exhaustion.

Then, to my surprise, the fellow turned round and came back towards me. As he did so, I noticed he was now carrying his heavy sack between two fingers of his left hand, swinging it jauntily as he did so. Before he had been almost doubled with its weight. As I came up to him he threw the sack at my feet, as if to say: 'So much for water bailiffs!' I opened the sack. It was stuffed only with straw, which I discovered is the normal Devon way of decoying the bailiff from the proper poachers, who in this instance were the three men who I had noticed were only mildly interested in my chase.

I showed my disappointment at the contents of the sack, whereupon my captive told me that if I wanted to see salmon caught out of the Torridge, I had better go and find Lew Cottell at the 'Blue Boar', in Bideford, 'for he's got a proper salmon fishing licence', he said, in tones of wonder and respect.

This was easier said than done. How is it that all professional fishermen look so much alike, that a description of one is useless? Why is it that so many professions produce similar personalities and appearances? The Devon fisherman with his wellingtons, thick blue sweater, heavily tobacco-stained moustache and accurate aim for the spittoon is no myth, but a realistic and platitudinous type. It is strange they should submit to this voluntary uniformity; but it is, of course, utilitarian, and I suppose it isn't surprising that they all have such leathery-looking faces and such sharp suspicious eyes.

My salmon expedition began to turn into a pub crawl as I searched through the 20 inns of Bideford, peering through the blue smoke for the elusive Mr Cottell. I did eventually catch up with him. He was dressed like any other fisherman, but there was this difference; he was not quaffing mild-and-bitter in the Public Bar, but sipping Hollands gin in the Saloon.

I asked him if he could take me salmon fishing one evening and offered him a drink. He agreed and ordered two more gins, which to my surprise he paid for. In order to account for this peculiar open-handedness, which is not a Devonian nor a fisherman's characteristic, I submitted myself to three hours of sitting in a small coracle-like boat on the Torridge during the middle of the night, for, as Cottell told me, that week the tides were running low, and it was midnight before he rowed out and set his nets across the river just below the old bridge.

Out came the bottle of gin. I now discovered the necessity for it, but I still could not explain how Cottell could afford it. As we sat there, he sipping the gin, I learned something of the ways of salmon.

Cottell spoke with strange respect for the fish. As he put it, 'There is something mysterious about salmon. They're not normal ordinary fish'. No one knows what happens to them after they have been up the rivers to spawn and cleanse themselves of sea lice on the gravel. After a few weeks they are free of parasites and then take to the sea again. While they are in the rivers they do not feed, I was told. They may rise to a fly, not through hunger, but from sheer irritation at this disturbance of their peace. If the salmon get caught above Weare Gifford and don't run back with the spring tide, they may stay there for months, and having lost their sea parasites, acquire river bugs behind the gills, which can suck all the blood out of a 15-pound salmon in a few weeks.

'Sometimes we go up there and carry them over the weir,' said Cottell. But what made him respect the fish was the mystery of where they disappear when they leave the rivers. Apparently no salmon are ever caught at sea, and it pleased Cottell to think of them returning each year to his own licensed preserves.

'But they won't be coming back for many more years if they devils over there are allowed to go on', he said, pointing to the tall chimney of the gas works silhouetted against the night, 'and if those fellows up at the milk factory go on cleaning their churns with disinfectant and pouring it into the river. Do ye know', he said to me very knowingly, while the breeze was scented with gin, 'one pint of milk in a thousand gallons of water will kill a salmon in less than ten minutes!'

A few minutes later he began to haul in the net. I was certainly not optimistic about seeing a salmon, but as the net came into the boat the water was broken by furious quick-silver, and as Cottell heaved I saw 12 great salmon thrashing. He received the whole thing with the nonchalance that comes from habit, and quickly began stowing the net away, and rowed back to the bank.

'How often do you get a catch like that?' I asked.

'Oh, most tides,' he replied, 'at this time of the year.'

Rapidly I worked it out in my head that with salmon about 10s. a pound, and the average weight of the salmon being 15 pounds, Cottell's ability to stand me gins was explained.

'You ought to be paying super tax', I suggested, 'with a profit like that.' A cautious, defiant look came into his eyes. 'We've got to pay for the licence, and that's five quid; and a net like this costs a couple of hundred.'

'Even so', I suggested, 'that leaves you a fair profit.'

'Fair enough, considering the chill the job gets into a man's marrow!'

And from Exmoor and Dartmoor, making their tortuous way through the narrow valley to the sea, run some very pretty trout streams. For the most part these are so overgrown that it is impossible to cast a fly. They are fished heavily by herons, and as few estates can now afford a water bailiff, the stock is being poached almost out of existence. The poachers are, in general, an integral part of Devon agriculture, and their methods are both ingenious and fascinating.

Whenever I have caught them in the act—a very difficult job indeed —I have been impressed by the fact that they regard this activity not as thieving, but as a legitimate rural sport. The poachers are seldom poor; they are often tenant farmers who drive away in a car. They are not prompted by hunger, as in the old days. To them, poaching is as much a sport as fox-hunting or beagling. And it carries its own code of honour—the true test of a sport. For instance, the genuine poacher will not trap or snare in the breeding season; he will often loose a cock bird; and he will not kill out of wanton destruction. This code makes the poacher distinct from the vandal. The latter is a thief without cunning or ingenuity.

Whereas the poacher will spend his evening plaiting the strands of black horsehair into a noose which he then ties on to a stick, and waits hours by the river bank till he can slip the hair noose over the trout head—an operation which may take him three or four hours—the vandal merely goes to a sheltered pool hidden in the woods with a bag of lime. His method is clumsy and the result is indiscriminate slaughter. He merely immerses the lime in the pool, forcing the suffocating fish to the surface, where they choke. From one pool the vandal may get half a dozen fair-sized trout: but at the same time he kills 40 or 50 small fishes which are not worth his picking up. These are left at the edge of the pool to show his contempt for efforts made to breed the fish. After such liming, I have even found dead fish 100 yards farther down the stream.

The land from Hartland Point to Bude is broken by innumerable valleys which used to contain derelict water-mills. The valleys are sheds of land about two miles long, generally flanked by self-sown woods of scrub oak, where all the trees have trunks like corkscrews, and the branches are shorn from the west with each twig pointing away from the cruel wind. As the valley approaches the sea, the woods give way to gorse, ling, and bracken: motionless buzzards hover over the great cliffs: gulls returning from the ploughland scissor the air out to sea.

12 Cliffs at Hartland Quay

Strangely enough, many Devon villages, whose population is only a tenth of the average market town, have lost this particular quality of being centred in their surrounding countryside. Old villages like Sticklepath no longer mine their copper; and they have no industry or market of their own to draw people to them, and have degenerated into little more than a row of petrol pumps. When the cars are not passing through them, these villages on the main road stand almost as barren and deserted as railway stations with no trains.

But villages off the main road, such as Hartland, still preserve an individual character. Although Hartland is of no great architectural beauty, except for its unnoticed Georgian vicarage and some trim eighteenth-century houses, it is still in touch with some of its past, though not as prosperous as when it contained the flourishing industries which were attached to the Abbey.

St Nectan's church reminds one of the old Welsh saint of that name who came across the Bristol Channel to convert the Devonians to Christianity—somewhat optimistically. The local legend is that he was beheaded at Newton Farm, as might have been expected; and that after his head fell to the ground the Saint himself picked it up and carried it to a certain stone, on which he placed it.

I think small villages like Hartland are at their best when their annual flower show or gymkhana is held. You would enjoy seeing the little stalls of sweet peas, long carrots and large onions, with their proud and beaming growers standing by their side; especially when the show is held in one of those enormous marquees which produce a strange greenish light. I like the gymkhana, with all its races for children; its sideshows, where you guess the weight of a pig and draw prizes from a bran tub, accompanied by a brass band which makes up for its lack of musical ability with a display of expectorating exuberance. Even so, you find to your surprise that the blare is charged with nostalgia.

I remember during the war, at the time of the Battle of Britain, Hartland still had its gymkhana, and nothing symbolised England's nerve more than this small carnival, so apparently oblivious of the aeroplanes overhead. I suppose it was the old story of Drake's game of bowls; a legend which can be verified, but not by scrabbling in the wormwood of history. If a legend is true you can be sure that its essential quality still exists. And the Devonian is at his best when he shows this almost sublime indifference to what are supposed to be world-shaking events. He has a confidence in his ability to overcome events, which, were it not proved by history to be a well-founded conceit, would be ludicrous.

I remember several incidents when the news was particularly bad; when the blitz was at its worst, and invasion seemed probable. Not for a second did the Devonian, who was armed with only a pitchfork, that anyhow he had mislaid, worry. He knew that he would set the matter 'arights' as he put it, though 'it might take a brave bit of time'. I really believe that this quality of almost insane self-assurance is the Devonian's principal attribute. It produced a Drake and a Raleigh, and I dare say the self-confidence of Churchill was derived from his Devonian ancestors. There is a point where confidence is vanity and vanity is stupidity. In Devon they are indistinguishable.

Before you leave Hartland, you must go down to the Quay. Not for the hotel there, though it has its site to commend it, and was built to house coastguards. The hill down is very steep. But in spite of this warning, go down to the Quay to look at the bones, the ribs of this planet we wander about on for a time. Buildings, churches and monuments may impress you, but the sight of these rocks will affect you in a different way. Buildings show us what hands can make, but rocks like these depict what time itself carves. They give you what can be called a cosmic realisation. Similar strata and formations can be seen at other places along the North Devon coast where the brows of the cliffs are furrowed with granite and scowl with slate. But it is silly to indulge in a pathetic fallacy about these rocks: they are beyond all human concepts: it is ridiculous to say they are cruel or beautiful. They are what they are. But somehow they tell us too what we are; gnats. These rocks are something to contemplate. They make important things seem trivial and simple things serious.

From Hartland, I must move you in the direction of Dartmoor. Though North Devon has more to offer, you have no time to spare. I suggest you drive to Okehampton, via Meddon, Dinworthy, Bradworthy, Sutcombe, Milton Damerel, Shebbear and Hatherleigh. This road takes you through the backwoods of Devonshire. It is country which is not famous for any feature, and this is its good fortune. Nobody goes there but the inhabitants, the postman, the milk lorry and the vet. But follow them; I suspect this undramatic scenery will captivate you. It does not try to sell you anything, not even its own beauty.

The Parish Church of John the Baptist at Hatherleigh is one of the most pleasing in Devonshire. This is due to its proportions rather than to any particular item it contains, though particular notice should be taken of the ninth-century Saxon font, and also the Norman font which is still complete with a beautiful wooden canopy. The stained glass windows are admirable, and a rare example of seventeenth-century Dutch glass is on the left of the main entrance. The single column of granite is reminiscent of the church at Chagford and probably also came from Dartmoor. Part of the roof is still painted and shows the original decorations which were removed from most churches during the seventeenth century. Several old cottages around the churchyard are worth noticing. Hatherleigh High Street contains examples of domestic architecture of most periods from the fourteenth to the present century, all within 200 yards.

FIVE

Dartmoor

There are two Hatherleighs: the quiet little town you see for six days of the week and the busy place you find on market days. Its cattle market is one of the busiest in North Devon. Then, on Market Day the High Street resembles Abilene. Bellowing bullocks are thwacked in and out of lorries; there are the cries and patter of the auctioneers, the slow drawl of the be-gaitered farmers; it is then like a set of a Western film. This similarity has, unfortunately, been exploited by the owners of one of the old pubs in the High Street, who have renamed it the 'Rodeo Inn' and decorated it like a Saloon of 1890 Texas. This vulgar attempt to attract tourists succeeds in embarrassing some locals. But a genuine coaching inn, the 'George', stands opposite and has not been tampered with. There are few inns of this type left with coach-yard and stables still intact and not yet turned into tea rooms. A place like the 'George' should be scheduled as an Ancient Monument.

Hatherleigh originally belonged to Tavistock Abbey. Some of the Commoners who still graze the moor believe that this right was given to them by John of Gaunt and have been known to quote the rhyme;

> *I, John of Gaunt, do give and do grant*
> *Hatherleigh Moor*
> *To Hatherleigh poor*
> *For evermore.*

After leaving Hatherleigh take the secondary road to Jacobstow where the small village church is worth looking at. But the most interesting feature around here is the timber which strangely has been left standing. You will see many oak trees along the road. Several must be 600 or 700 years old.

The next village in this direction is Sampford Courtenay where you will notice a wonderful panorama of Dartmoor above you.

North Tawton, a little further on, has many excellent examples of small Georgian houses in the main street. Some have been turned into village shops and are worth preserving. The road leads to Spreyton and then on to Whiddon Down through rich parkland country surrounding Moretonhampstead. The stone walls of the moors are still visible. You will feel the contrast of Dartmoor on one side with this narrow strip of parkland on the other.

After Spreyton and Whiddon Down I must lead you back along the edge of Dartmoor via Sticklepath to Okehampton. Just outside the old market town you will find an avenue of beech which surround the twelfth-century castle. This ruin, on its typical commanding position, is worth a visit.

Okehampton is, of course, proud and conscious of its Norman castle, but I think it should be more pleased with its perfectly proportioned Town Hall. Unhappily, judging by the value which the Urban Council have put on the delightful St James's Church, which stands only 100 yards away, I doubt whether they value the design of either by all the notices which leer over the entrance to this little church. One reads *Public Convenience*, though I do not suppose it refers to the church itself, and the other, which may do so, is inscribed *No Entry*.

As if this were not enough, the side of the small church bears a bus timetable board, a telephone kiosk, a letter-box, a bench, and a litter-bin. Somebody should go round the country awarding prizes for these examples of bumbledom.

But there is little else in Okehampton itself of any interest beyond a pub or two which have been open for three centuries. Do not be tempted to try and have a meal anywhere in this ancient borough. If you do, in all probability you will be told that lunch is not served after 2.0 or tea is not served after 4.15. Your best plan is to turn off at the road indicating the way to the station and proceed a mile until you reach the gate leading into the Dartmoor National Park. You will question my advice no doubt when first you see the hideous Army Camp at the entrance. But take heart and drive on round the circuit which will take you for about ten miles over the moor.

You will be amazed by the sudden and complete change of scenery. Within half a mile, it is as though you had entered an entirely different country. Indeed, Dartmoor with its tawny manelike colouring is partially reminiscent of some parts of Spain; and with its rolling lines broken by granite outcrops it recalls the South African veldt. It is beautiful, but as inhospitable as the moon. The few sheep and wild ponies graze among the heather and bracken; there is not a single croft and surprisingly enough no deer, grouse, partridge or even a hare.

You will wonder why Dartmoor is allowed to waste like this and why it is not stocked with game or planted with trees. I suppose one answer is that the Army have a lien on it for target practice and the prison authorities at Princetown prefer not to have too many trees on the moor to give cover to escaping prisoners.

This circuit round the National Park brings you back to the gate near the camp. I suggest you then keep to the secondary road and go in the direction of Gidleigh, passing the old copper mine on the Okehampton–Exeter road. Gidleigh, too, has its Norman castle and a Parish Church adjoining, with an interesting painted screen, Norman tower and porch.

Go on in the direction of Chagford along a lane bordering the stream then cross the old stone bridge and make for the 'Three Crowns Hotel'. This is a thirteenth-century monastery which became a pub soon after the Reformation. The outside of the building has, by some miracle, not been ruined by renovators and still stands in remarkably fine condition. Two fireplaces in the bars are worth looking at with their enormous granite lintels. But unfortunately both the kitchen and the refectory have been renovated beyond recognition. The outside of this pub is probably the best piece of architecture of this period in the county. The Parish Church across the road has a remarkably fine roof and all the pillars carrying the structure are single blocks of granite hewn from Dartmoor. The screen is modern but of traditional Devon design and painted in the original colours. The chapel is dedicated to St Catherine, the patron saint of tin miners. Chagford was made one of the Stannary towns in 1328.

Like Bideford the town has an unassuming, quiet dignity about it. It is unspoiled and centred. It can be proud of the fact that the nineteenth century did not stamp it with its commercialism or the twentieth century debauch it with concrete.

One of the things about Chagford, which I am sure you will notice, is the position of the graveyard. It is in the very centre of the town, which has grown up around the church, and consequently the grave-stones can be seen from every part of the square. As you stand in the bar of the hotel you can read the inscriptions on the tombs across the road. They have not railed the graveyard off or hidden it by a thick yew hedge, or done anything to pretend that death does not exist. Nor, like most towns, have they moved their graveyard to the out-skirts, somewhere near a refuse pit. It is a small point, but it does indicate that towns like Chagford have some philosophical attitudes and values which are becoming rare in so-called progressive cities. I cannot imagine what the dwellers of Los Angeles would make of Chag-ford's simple gravestones in the middle of the town. They would be profoundly shocked both by the simplicity and the proximity.

From Chagford go in the direction of Ashburton. This road will take you over Dartmoor again. On the horizon you will see what you might mistake for the ruins of ancient castles or primitive fortifications, but they are not, they are outcrops of granite piling up to the Tors.

Beauty is seldom comforting. It may be excessively cruel: and where the bones of the granite stick through the poor soil on Dart-moor, one gets a definite feeling of relentlessness: and wherever the horizon seems to roll away from you like an ocean of land, one receives an impression of a wilderness. And how many of us can stand living in a wilderness without becoming oppressed by its loneliness? Although we have laid all the phantoms of headless horses and baying hounds which used to haunt Yes Tor and Brown Willie, why do we still flee across this desolate plateau? Is it that we are running from ourselves, the ghosts that we have become?

Most of us, if left alone on this wilderness, would fail to find any

14 Chagford Church: typical Devon barrel-
shaped roof

comfort in the rolling heather or ling, or the quaint stone-built farm-houses; but might in desperation seek the companionship of the prison at Princetown in preference to the loneliness of the liberty outside. This is not to say that Dartmoor is not beautiful, but to warn people that beauty is not to be confused with prettiness. It can be most disquieting.

You will be fascinated by the old stone walls built with lumps of granite which must have taken four men to lift into position. These walls have stood for centuries. No cement or mortar keeps them together. They are not only monuments to cheap labour, but to people who made things not only for themselves but for generations to follow.

Crossing Dartmoor and finding oneself suddenly surrounded by its unfriendly desolation I am reminded of a line of Tennyson, for here

Shadows of the world appear.

It is as if one had suddenly been transported on a time machine into a prehistoric world where cruelty was one dimension and loneliness the other measurement of man. I find I can easily believe the seventeenth-century description of the moor; 'wolves and winged serpents are no strangers to its hills and valleys'. These feelings are of course induced because we have become so gregarious and because Dartmoor is now almost uninhabited. This was not always the case. When the moor was a forest it was closely peopled. Remains of primitive dwellings in pounds show that if we allow six persons to have dwelt in each hut over 2,000 people must once have inhabited an area of less than a square mile. From the number of flint skin-scrapers found on the moor it must have been an excellent hunting ground before the Bronze Age. And it was certainly well populated during that period and right up to the decline of the Devon tin-mining industry in the nineteenth century. It was not the bogs or the winged serpents which depopulated Dart-moor but the discovery of tin in Malaya and Bolivia and the import of cheap wool from Australia.

At one time, the moor had a great number of pagan religious struc-tures similar no doubt to Stonehenge and Avebury. But most of these antiquities were either demolished by the Christians, who used the

5 *Grimspound: prehistoric site on Dartmoor*

granite to build their own churches as at Chagford, or they were carted off to be used for farmhouse lintels, gate-posts or bridges. But enough remain as at Grimspound to show that the moor was once a place like Salisbury Plain, of particular religious significance—no doubt because it was high ground.

Legends are the principal crop on Dartmoor. Some are quite memorable, such as that of the Childe of Plymstock, who was a large landowner in the reign of Edward III. Having no heirs, he made a will bequeathing his lands to whichever church he should be buried in. One day when out hunting in the Dartmoor forest he lost his way in the snow. Whereupon to protect himself from exposure he had an extremely practical notion: he killed his horse, disembowelled it and crept inside its carcase. He died, in spite of this. However, before expiring, he wrote a message in his own blood;

> *He that finds and brings me to my tomb*
> *My land of Plymstock shall be his doom.*

Then ensued a battle over the body between the monks of St Rumon's and the parishioners of Plymstock. The monks found the body and were carrying it off, and the Plymstockians lay in wait for them by the only bridge over the stream in their path. The monks, however, got wind of this, and improvising a bridge over the stream lower down, got safely to Tavistock with the corpse.

Another legend relates to the last male heir of the Dowrich family of Sandford, who was killed by a fall from his horse one winter night when returning home drunk. Since then, his ghost has been ascending the hill to the house at the rate of a cock's stride every moon. In the course of this journey he has to cross a bridge as narrow and sharp as the edge of a sword, and every time he falls into the stream he has to go back to the beginning again. When, if ever, he reaches his former dwelling, dire misfortune is supposed to fall on the inmates.

Perhaps the most famous Devonshire legend is that of Tom Pearse. Who was Tom Pearse? Nobody knows, though most people have heard of his old grey mare and the gormless rustics, including 'Uncle Tom Cobbleigh and all', who collectively mounted the poor beast's sagging back 'for to go to Widdecombe Fair'. Somewhat naturally the weight of these nine riders proved too much for the mare, 'who was took sick and died' and as the old ballad reports, they never returned in the flesh, though;

> *When the wind whistles cold on the moor of a night,*
> *All along, down along, out along, lee,*
> *Tom Pearse's old mare doth appear ghastly white,*
> *Wi' Bill Brewer, Jan Stewer, Peter Gurney,*
> *Peter Davy, Dan'l Whiddon, Harry Hawk,*
> *Old Uncle Tom Cobbleigh and all.*

In fact there are few legends which account for quite so many ghosts being seen at one and the same time. But it is not quite clear whether they are still on their way to the fair, or in the dilatory process of returning.

Widdecombe-in-the-Moor is rather like the village of Bray on the Thames, in that both places are known the world over wholly on account of old ballads. As the very sound of the word Widdecombe suggests, it is a typical South Devon market town, nestling in a valley which is a fold of Dartmoor. It is one of those old villages which one often finds in the West Country. They are dignified yet unassuming; humble in each particular dwelling, but proud when viewed as a whole. They appear idle to the visitor; yet to the inhabitant they are hives of busy gossip, if not industry itself. And to my mind, the most vivid impression which such places as Widdecombe give is their careless awareness of their own past: they do not flaunt it at you: yet they do not let you forget it. They are so confident of their history that they do not boast about their antiquity. Indeed, such places are so aware of their past that they do not think the matter worth mentioning.

Consequently, when you are in Widdecombe, or attending its fair, although you stand in what may well be almost a medieval street, and participate in one of the oldest carnivals in the country, you may be sure of this: nobody will mention the fact. For, as I say, Widdecombe is too old a place to count her years; and if she could she would not publicise them, for such matters would not be in keeping with her essential modesty, which amounts to an inarticulate but strong sense of propriety and decorum.

Widdecombe Fair arose when the sheep and ponies used to be driven
in from the moor in the autumn. Michaelmas is still the season when
most farm rents fall due; and consequently that was the time when
the sheep farmers used to sell off some of their spring-born lambs to
be fattened down on the South Hams. The herds of wild ponies would
be thinned out so that the rest might just manage to survive the winter.
It is the same at Bampton Fair, where the ponies were driven down to
the villages from Exmoor eventually to find their way to the coal
mines. I suppose Widdecombe could claim that it has had a fair as
long as there has been a rough moor at its back, breeding shaggy sheep
and sturdy ponies.

And I dare say this year Mr Dunn, a local resident of Widdecombe, will once again delight the children by dressing up in an
old linen smock and riding his old grey mare across the village
green. And as usual, the old custom of putting several riders on
one horse's back will be observed by letting three or four small
riders go down on her back to the field where the children's sports
are held.

And no doubt—for it would be as difficult to change a Widdecombe
custom as to turn the bleak wind from the moor—the famous tug-of-
war will be pulled again on the green, and the *Uncle Tom Cobbleigh
Challenge Cup* filled with foaming beer to its brim. The whole fair is
very modest, but as genuine as the moor itself.

Not far from Ashburton is the Abbey of Buckfast. It was founded in the
reign of Henry II on the site of a Benedictine Abbey which existed in
Saxon times. It was partially destroyed at the Dissolution, except for
the Tithe Barn, but in 1882 the Abbey was bought for a colony of
monks from Burgundy who rebuilt the monastery and the church. The
present buildings are of no particular architectural interest; and it is a
sign of these commercial times that in order to maintain themselves
the monks appear to be extremely busy in producing various brands
of toffee under the Abbey trade name. They also bottle the honey
which you can buy in any town in Devonshire.

A few miles away is the village of Dean Prior where the poet Herrick had the living after he left London. Herrick was a cockney, and

grumbled about 'dull Devonshire'. He missed the company of Ben Jonson and the 'Tribe of Ben'.

He was ejected from his living during the Protectorate and replaced by one John Syme, a Puritan, but was reinstated after the Restoration, remaining there until his death in 1674. The story is that he once threw his sermon at the congregation and cursed them for inattention; it is also said that he kept a pet pig, which he taught to drink cider out of a tankard.

However, Herrick was not very complimentary to Devonshire in his poems: any profit he may have gained from the countryside is only shown indirectly in his lyrics.

> *Before I went*
> *In banishment*
> *Into the loathed West,*
> *I could rehearse*
> *A lyric verse,*
> *And speak it with the best.*

The Devonians are referred to elsewhere as:

> *A people currish; churlish as the seas;*
> *And rude (almost) as rudest Savages.*

which lines are surely eligible for an Anthology of Bad Poetry.

Of course, Herrick is only remembered for the few poems in anthologies, such as: 'Gather ye rosebuds while ye may', but he deserves more consideration than is generally accorded him. His importance is that Ben Jonson introduced him to classic models. One could say that Herrick is one of the rungs on the ladder which leads from Jonson, Marvel, Rochester and Dryden to Pope.

From Buckfastleigh there is a small road which leads up to the moor again via Holne then on to Poundsgate and the famous beauty spot of Dartmeet which leads on to Two Bridges. Both of these places are worth visiting if you are on Dartmoor in the spring or autumn, but they are to be avoided during the holiday months when they are mere car parks.

Do not waste your time visiting Princetown. It is known only for its

17 Buckfast Abbey : rebuilt this century

prison. Instead, drive towards Tavistock and before you reach the town turn right to Cudlipptown then head for Lydford.

Lydford is one of the mysteries of Devonshire. Today you will find a very dull little place with nothing more to it than a school, three or four shops and a bus stop. You will notice a National Trust board indicating the way down to Lydford Gorge, and as you descend into this you will pass the remains of a Norman castle, which was built in the twelfth century on the site of a Saxon fortification. The castle consists of nothing more than a few feet of walls of the keep. The Gorge is picturesque, and you might wonder why it has not been dammed to power a turbine at the bottom, but that is all you can see of Lydford today. But this is the town which was once the rival of Exeter, the largest borough in Devonshire, and prosperous long before Exeter and Plymouth. It was once the site of the Saxon Mint and the *Saxon Chronicle* reports that it was sufficiently important for the Danes to invade it in 997.

Yet even after this its prosperity was such that the town grew up again, so that by the time of Domesday it was the most populated place in the whole county.

Yet nothing remains. Certainly one cannot see why Lydford was ever so important. True, it stands in a natural defensive position; the Gorge and the castle might have made it almost impregnable. Perhaps it was just this strength which brought about its downfall? We know that Lydford withstood the blandishment of William the Conqueror for a time, unlike Exeter, which let discretion open the gates after a brief show of valour. Perhaps Lydford with a more natural position of fortification was encouraged to a kind of arrogance which irritated the Conqueror, and it may be the town was finally destroyed because of its show of resistance to the Normans. Yet even so, because of its position on Dartmoor it received the appointment as Chief Stannary town and 'Lydford Law' is still a phrase in the language.

The production of tin from Dartmoor was so important to the Crown that the miners were able to obtain many licences and privileges; these consisted of their own Courts and their own officers functioning at Lydford. Ordinary Courts could not touch them.

I oft have heard of Lydford Law
How in the morn they hang and draw
And sit in judgment after
At first I wonder at it much,
But now I find their reasons such
That it deserves no laughter.

Lydford Law made a contribution to English Law, when a man called
Strode was imprisoned 'in the foul and detestable dungeon at Lydford',
and since he was Member for Plympton his sentence was quashed.
This led to the declaration of the right of Parliamentary free speech.
But, as the poet William Browne remarked:

There is a bridge, there is a Church,
Seven ashes and an oak.
Three houses standing and ten down.

There is a local tradition that Lydford Law originated with Jeffreys
during the Bloody Assizes, but it obviously pre-dates that. There is
also a tradition that Jeffreys' ghost haunts the castle in the shape of a
pig. This is probably true.

Dartmoor has few roads. As I want you to cross the moor again it
will be necessary for you to double back to Tavistock and then take
the road to Two Bridges and head for Moretonhampstead. I suggest
you do this because I want you to be in the right position to explore
South Devon. That is from the east down the Teign Valley. I do not
think you will regret crossing the moor again, especially if you arrange
to do it at night when the moon is up. It is quite a frightening place
then, particularly when the wind is on the leash. To do this journey
may mean you will have to dine at Tavistock. I admit this presents
some difficulty. For as I have discovered, some of the inns of Tavistock
are run on the lines of boarding schools—perhaps a little stricter.
Though they do not fine you if you enter the dining-room after 8.45,
they simply refuse to serve you at all. If you are punctual, you have
the more cause for regret.

Tavistock was an important Saxon town and a centre of population
long before the Norman Conquest. It is supposed to have been founded
by Ordulf. He is one of the semi-mythical heroes of the Saxons which

have an equivalent in every race; that is, a man with the strength of a giant able to cross a river with one stride and fell an ox with one blow. The Abbey itself was founded about 960 and 30 years later was destroyed by the Danes when they also laid waste to Lydford. The Abbey was large and very wealthy: but it is doubtful whether the legend is true that it could house 1,000 men. But it is not Ordulf who interests me so much as his sister, Elfryth. It is strange that she has never become the subject of an opera. Saxon history records that she was a woman of great beauty. King Edgar, hearing of her reputation, sent a noble from his Court called Aeoelwold to view her and report back if she were beautiful enough for him to make her his queen. Apparently instead of making a dispassionate survey, the unlucky man fell in love with her himself. He went back to the Court, reported that the woman was plain and later asked permission to marry her himself. This consent was given. Aeoelwold returned to Devon and married her. Things went well for a time till a few years later the King announced his intention of visiting the county. The husband, now fearing the consequence of his deceit, confessed everything to his wife and begged her to make herself look as unattractive as he had reported she was. Not unnaturally Elfryth, who had now had some years as a Devon housewife, decided to do the opposite and to make herself as beautiful as she could for the King. His Majesty came and immediately saw that the woman should have been his Consort. Aeoelwold was conveniently killed the following day in an accident while out hunting with the Monarch. His widow mounted the throne. Subsequently her son became one of the Patrons of Tavistock Abbey and it was due to this royal interest that it became the greatest religious house in Devonshire.

Tavistock was so wealthy that in the fourteenth century the monks already had a reputation for sloth, luxury and gluttony. Pope Leo X granted it a Bull exempting the Abbey from Episcopal Jurisdiction, but a quarter of a century later its day was over, and the Abbey and all its possessions fell into the hands of a grasping merchant called Russell who, of course, was the ancestor to the Dukes of Bedford, who still own the place. This change of ownership which has been whitewashed by historians under the name of the Reformation was not wholly to the country's advantage. Though it is only fair to state that the Russells have been good landlords. Yet it is clear that the Abbey had acted as a bastion for learning in a vast sea of ignorance. Its loss has never been filled. The monks were maligned; they were obviously given to more than sloth and luxury; indeed, they ran the first printing press in England. Two works printed here still exist, the first a copy of Boethius's *Consolations of Philosophy* translated by Walter of Osney, dated 1525: the second is a copy of *The Statutes of the Stannaries*, dated 1534.

Unhappily, practically nothing of the Abbey buildings remains and possibly less of their tradition of learning. In the last century an enterprising spiv called Saunders built over the site and with the materials belonging to the ruins constructed the monstrous 'Bedford Hotel'.

It was of course not strange that the Abbey printed *The Statutes of the Stannaries* since Tavistock was the chief mining centre in Devonshire. As you enter the town today you will see a large notice on the road bearing the inscription, 'Stannary Town'. This confuses many visitors. Tin has enriched Tavistock; one mine, which was sunk with a capital of £1,000 in the last century, paid a million and a quarter in dividends. The mines are not so prosperous today, though with an unsettled future in Malaya they would seem to have possibilities. All geologists agree that there is more tin still in the ground than was ever taken out.

You cannot fail to notice the rather ungainly statue of Sir Francis Drake that stands in the centre of the town. Drake was born in a cottage at Crowndale in 1539. As one of the great British worthies Drake deserves something better than this poor statue. He was one of the greatest navigators and explorers of all time: that we had several such people in the Elizabethan era does not seem sufficient excuse for our treatment of their achievements so casually.

Drake first took to the sea under his kinsman, Sir John Hawkins. They both suffered from Spanish treachery at San Juan de Ulloa and from that day decided to wage war on Spain whether the Queen declared it or not. Drake's first expedition was when he took Vera Cruz. In 1577, he sailed from Plymouth on what was to be one of the most remarkable voyages ever undertaken. He had glimpsed the Pacific

Ocean when in Mexico and decided then to find his way round to it. He had five ships, though they were so small they hardly deserved that name. The largest was only 120 tons: yet with these coracles he set out to sail round the world. In spite of desertion, scurvy and every possible kind of accident and misfortune, he achieved his object and sailed back to Plymouth in 1580. For this incredible feat of navigation, courage and fortitude, he received the same honour we now give to footballers and owners of holiday camps, and was knighted by the Queen. After this, Drake continued to harass the Spaniards and took a great deal of booty from them. It is said that the Queen herself was a shareholder in these expeditions. At any rate there is some evidence to suggest that her disapproval was allayed by the gift of an occasional pendant. While on one of these voyages Drake's fiancée decided that it is better to have all of the wrong man than half of the right one. While he was at sea she tired of that rival and decided to marry some yeoman farmer. The legend is that she was actually on her way to church when she heard Drake's Drum sound in Plymouth Bay. She then ran to meet him.

His most famous exploit of all was, of course, when he sailed into Cadiz harbour performing the exploit which he lightly dismissed as 'singeing the King of Spain's beard'. It was a strategic master-stroke and destroyed a large part of the Spanish navy. Drake had initiative, also the advantage over contemporary admirals of not being in wireless communication with Whitehall. His whole career was, of course, a prelude to the sailing of the Armada. He was appointed Vice-Admiral of the Fleet, which assembled in Plymouth Sound to await the invasion. He then brushed them up the Channel and destroyed what had been considered invincible. His last voyage was also in companionship with Hawkins when they sailed for the West Indies in 1595. Hawkins died within a few weeks, Drake within a few months. I doubt if the Greeks had better heroes than these, but nobody writes their Odyssey. The best we do is to name a teashop after them.

The poet William Browne was born in Tavistock in 1591. He was a friend of Drayton, Selden and Ben Jonson, and was known as 'Sweet Willy of the Western Main'. He was the author of an *Elegy on the Death of Prince Henry*, a collection of poems entitled *Britannia's Pastorals*, and the masque *Ulysses and Circe*. He is also reputed to be the author of the following epitaph on the Countess of Pembroke:

> Underneath this sable hearse
> Lies the subject of all verse,
> Sidney's sister, Pembroke's mother;
> Death! Ere thou hast slain another,
> Learned and fair, and good as she,
> Time will throw a dart at thee.

Of course, this is almost certainly by Ben Jonson.

Other literary figures of this area include William Gifford, a considerable satirist of the late eighteenth and early nineteenth century, who influenced Byron; and John Wolcot, who wrote under the name of Peter Pindar, a rival and contemporary of Gifford, whose verse was scurrilous but indifferent.

Now with the doubtful delicacies of Tavistock within you, you must brave the moor again. Make sure you have enough petrol. Do not drive too fast: you can come across a herd of moor ponies in the middle of the road. I hope there is sufficient moon up to make the Tors appear menacing, enough mist to reflect your headlamps at times. I do not doubt that it will be raining. If you are feeling brave, stop the car in the middle of the moor and just sit there to listen to the wind as it flees from itself dragging a granite shadow: not every worthwhile experience is necessarily pleasant.

SIX

South Devon

I assume (perhaps a little late) that before leaving Tavistock you had
the forethought to telephone an hotel at Moretonhampstead to book
a room for the night and to warn them to keep their front door open
until 11 p.m. On that assumption you will have had a good night and
be refreshed to see something of South Devon.

I do not think you will find very much to interest you in Moretonhampstead itself. It is a prosperous market town. That is all you will see.
I suggest you drive down the Teign Valley via Lustleigh and Bovey
Tracey. I think you will enjoy the scenery with Dartmoor scowling
above you on your right but the fertile valley in front to reassure you.
In the change here Devon is at its most versatile; within a few miles
the bleak moor gives way to the most luxurious parkland, well-
watered pastures, and thickly wooded hills. It is a generous country.

Moretonhampstead itself is a busy market town and appears to
belong to the land surrounding it. It contains several old inns, not yet
debauched by tourism. You will notice that a great deal of the houses
are still thatched and that the thatch is in good condition. This is
probably the last generation who will see this kind of roofing or be able
to admire the skill put into it. But remember, without thatch there will
be fewer fires. Moretonhampstead exudes an air of rural prosperity.
That is to say the shops indicate that there is plenty of money in the
district, but like so many parts of Devonshire where there is material
well-being, they could also be classed as depressed areas in a cultural
sense. By which I mean that none of these prosperous towns, including
Newton Abbot which is the next on the way to Torquay, has a theatre,

19 *Moretonhampstead: on the edge of Dartmoor*

an art gallery, or a concert hall. Their cultural life used to revolve round the church; these are now empty. One can say truthfully that people have now become obsessed with two machines, cash registers and TV sets, and their lives are a busy sleepwalk between these two gadgets. This somnambulism gives an impression of poverty and deadness behind the façade of prosperity.

Newton Abbot has now almost joined on to Torquay as Torquay has joined to Paignton. I suggest you go on to Teignmouth, a pleasant little seaport. It suffered the last invasion which England sustained in 1690 when the French landed 1,700 men and sacked the town. Keats wrote his poem *Isabella* here, though his comments are unlikely to commend the place:

> You may say what you will of Devonshire, but the truth is it is a splashy, rainy, misty, snowy, foggy, haily, floody, A muddy, slip-shod county. The hills are very beautiful—when you get a sight of 'em. The primroses are out, but then you, perforce, are in: the cliffs are of a fine deep colour, but then the clouds are constantly vieing with them. I fancy the air to be of a deteriorating quality.

It is usual to mention only buildings which are notable for their beauty but there are two in Teignmouth which are really worth looking at because of their extreme ugliness. They are collectors' pieces. One is the Catholic and the other the Congregational church. They are separated by less than 100 yards in the centre of Teignmouth and both are fine examples of the worst architecture in Europe. We have had museums of fine art, perhaps we should start museums of bad art?

Dawlish, the next town along the coast, grew up from smuggling but from this relatively honest occupation it has degenerated into a purveyor of knicknacks to caravanners. This is a pity, because it is well situated and has a pleasant combe. In 1810 the town was almost entirely destroyed by a sudden torrent of water descending the valley from Haldon and washing everything out to sea in a similar manner to what happened at Lynmouth in the 1950s.

From Dawlish you can avoid returning on the coast road by heading inland to Ashcombe, then going to Bishopsteignton to cross the river again at the mouth. You will enjoy the magnificent sweep of Babbacombe Bay and seeing Torquay ahead of you, you will think that is the place to lunch.

Although Torquay is not an old town and only dates back a couple of hundred years, it is the first known site of human life in England. The exploration of Kent's Cavern and Tornewton Cave at Torbyran has carried back the history of man in this country not only to Palaeolithic days, but to interglacial and even pre-glacial times. Though Torquay is one of the youngest towns in the country it is therefore the oldest known human settlement. Robert Ardrey, in his excellent book *African Genesis*, reports that the Tornewton Cave had a variety of occupants there in succeeding phases of the Pleistocene period. Five layers of deposit were excavated. The fifth and oldest had been made by cave bears, in a time of cold. It had been succeeded by a warm era, the fourth layer, when hyenas had made the cave their lair. Then in the third the cold had returned, and with it the bears again.

If calculations are correct, this hyena deposit had been made during the warm period about 130,000 years ago, between the last two glaciations, when Neanderthal Man was entering Europe and dropping the handaxes here and there to mark his open camp sites, when rhododendrons bloomed in high Alpine places and the hippopotamus flourished in Britain.

From an archaeological point of view this area is one of the most interesting in England. Even flint and bone weapons have been discovered from the submerged forest beds of Tor Bay. The town itself is remarkable for its continental appearance. It is reminiscent of many towns on the Riviera. The date palms on the front give this impression. When Napoleon was brought here for a few weeks on the *Bellerophon* on his way to exile at St Helena, he noticed this continental aspect and remarked, 'What a beautiful country, how much it resembles the capital Porto Ferrajo in Elba.'

Torquay is now a dormitory town mainly occupied by retired people living on pensions. These account for the large hotels and blocks of flats on the front. The only building of any great interest is Torre Abbey in the centre of the town which was founded in 1196. The Spanish Barn adjoining it still stands. One of the Armada ships was brought into the bay and the crew were imprisoned in the great barn. Of the abbey itself little remains but the gateway, which is a splendid structure.

After Torquay, get through Paignton as quickly as the traffic allows and go to Brixham.

Brixham is the best of South Devon. It is one of the few towns left with a *raison d'être* other than a parasitical existence on tourism. Brixham has two excellent harbours and these are filled not with speed-boats but genuine trawlers. Most of them look barely seaworthy, all of them are colourful, with their bright red and blue sails, and all that fascinating litter on their decks; scarlet nylon nets which the fishermen stand mending as dexterously as lace-makers; lobster pots; hunks of cork; coils of rope; boxes of fish and crates of ice. I suspect that you will be able to stand on the quay here and stare happily down by the hour watching the slow and leisurely way the fishermen prepare their gear for the next catch. And if the weather is calm you will want to go fishing yourself. Several boats at Brixham specialise in shark fishing and will take visitors out for a three-hour spell. Or, if you wish to have one of the best meals I know, go out mackerel fishing and, as soon as you return, grill the fresh fish on a bonfire. If mackerel does not appeal, there are lobsters and crabs in crates on the quay besides other slippery delights such as Dover soles, turbot and buckets of squids.

If you are tired of motoring, Brixham is the sort of place to stay for a few days: idly watching its activities from the quay will repair your own energies. The only thing I do not like in Brixham are the terrible shops which cater for visitors: they sell water-colours which have been painted by colour-blind gnomes, and what they call 'Art Pottery'. I am not sure what this means; could you have art poetry or art music? But I suppose the vendors are trying to indicate that these particular pots in their heavy curves and sombre colours have been designed not for use but for ornament. More's the pity.

Brixham was the site for the landing of William of Orange in 1688, when he claimed the throne of England. The local tradition is that when William approached the shore he asked if he was welcome. 'If

20 Brixham Harbour

I am,' he called out to those on the shore, 'then come and carry me in.' At which a stubby little man jumped into the water and did so. A family in the area still claims its relationship with this man who ferried William into his kingdom.

After leaving Brixham, I suggest you take the coast road and drive via Kingswear to Stoke Fleming where there is a beautiful little beach which by some strange miracle is unpolluted by those monstrosities of comfort and convenience which litter our shore.

Further along you will come to Strete where again you will find a splendid bathing beach adjoining the Nature Reserve for wildfowl. You will observe that here the shore is not even littered by a litter bin.

This beach road leads you on to Torcross and Frogmore where there are many beautiful walled farmhouses. Many of these buildings with their solid and domestic architecture which has, for the most part, been improvised, will give you more pleasure than the churches and other deliberately designed buildings.

At Kingswear, there is an antique shop by the road which is worth a visit before you cross on the ferry to Dartmouth. This too is a town which has grown by a river, is embraced by a river, and is given meaning because of that river. If you have time, hire a sailing boat and sail up the Dart. This is the way to see the best of Devon; from its rivers, not its roads.

The most dramatic view perhaps in the whole of Devonshire is of Dartmouth Castle, on the estuary of the Dart, with its splendid Norman keep, though most of the surviving building dates from the fifteenth century. During the thirteenth century Dartmouth was undoubtedly one of the five most important ports in England and was a naval base centuries before Plymouth. Henry VII ordered an iron chain to be held across the estuary whenever attack was imminent. It ran from the castle a quarter of a mile across the estuary to Kings Weir. During the day the chain lay on the bed of the river, but was raised at night. Dartmouth grew up around the castle which lost importance as soon as artillery made such fortifications ineffective. This dramatic building was the last sight of England which the occupants of the *Mayflower* saw

21 *The Buttermarket at Dartmouth*

as they left England for the New World. It was the point they looked for when the sailors returned from their voyages of discovery. For a time, Dartmouth was prosperous from the trade from the New World, losing this prosperity to Southampton, where the Solent was able to take boats of a greater tonnage.

If I have not been able to persuade you to hire any kind of a boat to see the Dart on the river itself, I urge you to loiter along the graceful banks by driving slowly and stopping frequently. Go right up the river via Cornworthy and Ashprington to Totnes and then go back on the other side of the river to Stoke Gabriel and go down to the old quay which is built across the estuary. The Dart is one of the most beautiful rivers in England and the quay is as good a vantage point as any I know. From here, bypass Totnes by going across country to Berry Pomeroy and Littlehampton, then join the river again and go on north to Dartington.

Dartington Hall was originally the home of the Champernownes, and was a gift of William the Conqueror to William de Falaise. It passed to the Duke of Exeter before the Champernownes acquired it in the reign of Elizabeth. The most striking feature of the Manor is the Hall, 70 feet long and 40 feet wide, and the quadrangle, which is very reminiscent of an Oxford or Cambridge College. And indeed, through the beneficence of Mrs Elmhurst, the present owner, Dartington Hall has become something of a university. Among other things, it contains a Drama and Ballet School, besides an advanced Forestry and Agricultural Division. It is one of the most enlightened centres in the county, or for that matter in the country, and has done much to integrate education with the locality and to act as a cultural centre, in the true sense, which is to be connected with those things which are growing about it. Consequently, it provides an advanced school of pottery worked with Devon clay, woodworking shops which manufacture furniture from lumber grown on the estate, besides a weaving mill for the wool produced from the surrounding hills. The farm attached to the manor has led the county in many agricultural experiments. Dartington provides the kind of cultural lead which used to be found in the monasteries. You will be able not only to get a meal at this oasis, but also to do some shopping at the estate store. But if you do not eat here, there is, a few miles up the river, a small unpretentious little café by the bank called 'Salmon Leap'. They actually serve local salmon for luncheon and it is not overcooked.

I am quite sure you will enjoy exploring the river Dart either by boat or by coasting along its bank to spending your time visiting all the built-up coastal area round Start or Bigbury Bay. This coast must have been very beautiful before 1920. Now it is only a matter of a generation before Torquay and Plymouth will be joined.

There is a fast road to Plymouth just by the 'Salmon Leap', but you can leave it at Dean and thread your way across the side roads via North Huish, Ugborough, Ermington and Westlake. This way will bring you into Plymouth via Plympton.

Plymouth is the most renowned town in Devonshire, and the largest, though its growth is recent. It is not even mentioned in the *Saxon Chronicle* and was only a hamlet at the time of Domesday, and not even called Plymouth then, but Sutton. In eight centuries the population has increased 2,500 times. But like Torquay, which has also grown very rapidly and yet has no medieval history, Plymouth yields abundant evidence that it was a centre of population in the Stone Age. From the gold and silver coins which have been unearthed it is quite clear, too, that this district was thriving at the period immediately preceding the Roman invasion. The Romans themselves left no remains here.

The legend that Plymouth was one of the ports with which the Phoenicians traded in tin cannot be substantiated.

During the fourteenth century Sutton was a small fishing village. The hamlet did not grow until the manor was acquired by a family called Valletorts, who encouraged the Prior of Plympton to develop the little harbour. The monastic orders, Carmelites, Franciscans and Dominicans, all contributed to its growth in the fourteenth century. At the siege of Calais, Plymouth was big enough to contribute more ships than any other town except Dartmouth.

Like many towns bordering an estuary on this coast, Plymouth was invaded by the French. In the last invasion in 1403, no fewer than 600 houses were burned and most of the population were either killed or taken prisoner. During the next two centuries the city was destroyed, like most towns in Devon, at least three times by great fires.

The town's fame rests on its association with the Elizabethan sailors, William Hawkins and, later, Drake. Hawkins was the first Englishman to sail into the Gulf of Mexico. He was probably born in 1532 and died on the last expedition he undertook with Drake in 1595. It could be said that an account of these voyages which sailed from Plymouth during the reign of Elizabeth would be almost a history of the foundation of the British Empire.

Drake ploughed a furrow round the world. It was to Plymouth he returned with his ship laden with blocks of gold and silver. Not unnaturally he was made Mayor, and represented the town in Parliament. It was from Plymouth that Drake sailed in 1587 to 'singe the King of Spain's beard'.

Plymouth is still grateful to Drake because, like many Elizabethan sailors, he was a man of many parts and was as able a surveyor as he was a navigator. It was he who constructed the land water-leat from the river Medway, which still supplies the city, and without which it could never have grown. Drake's memory is still drunk at the annual inspection of the Waterworks by the Corporation of Plymouth. Under his portrait in the Guild Hall there are these lines:

> *Who, with fresh streams, refreshed this town that first,*
> *Was kissed with waters, yet did pine for thirst.*

And it was from Plymouth that Drake and Hawkins sailed with 190 vessels to resist the Spanish Armada.

The much-cherished story that, when news of the approach of the Armada was brought, Drake was playing bowls on the Hoe and insisted on finishing his game, remarking 'There's time enough to play the game out, and thrash the Spaniards afterwards', is probably apocryphal. Even if it is untrue, it is worth repeating because it is typical of that Devonian self-confidence which can still be found today. The defeat of the Armada is still celebrated in Plymouth by the ringing of church bells on 25 July, when the Mayor and Corporation walk in state to the service.

The prosperity that Plymouth acquired in the Elizabethan era was

almost destroyed by the outbreak of plague in the reign of Charles I,
when a third of the population died within a few months.

Its next and probably most important contribution to history is the
part it played in the settlement of New England, when the Plymouth
Company was formed. This Company originated in the patents that
were granted by Elizabeth to Raleigh to settle in Virginia. Raleigh
spent £40,000 in an attempt to plant colonies in this territory. Five
times he sent ships to Virginia to maintain the garrisons at the City of
Raleigh which he had founded. These attempts to colonise Virginia
failed; most of the inhabitants were killed by the natives or went native
themselves.

But greater success was achieved in 1620 when a new Charter was
granted to the Plymouth Company 'for the planning, ruling and govern-
ing of New England in America'. The patentees of this Company were
the Duke of Lennox, the Marquis of Buckingham, the Earls of Arundel
and Warwick, Sir Ferdinando Gorges and 34 other people. Without
doubt it was Sir Ferdinando Gorges who was the moving spirit behind
this Company, and he was the most effective coloniser of America.

The Charter gave the Company all property and control over 'all
North America from the Atlantic to the Pacific between the 40th and
48th degrees of North latitude'. This grant was too vast to be realised
and merely allowed a free-for-all in which Gorges appropriated the
whole of Maine for himself, and all of New Hampshire for a friend.
Before this Company disintegrated, it had granted a Charter to the
city of Massachusetts.

On 6 September 1620, without any concession from the Plymouth
Company and without a warrant from the King, the *Mayflower* sailed
from Plymouth. The Pilgrims intended to head for the Hudson, but
landed in the territory of the Plymouth Company, and there founded
New Plymouth. But it is a mistake to assume that the people of the
Mayflower were all Devonians. Most of them came from East Anglia.
It is possible some of the crew were Devonians. We know that Tre-
lawney and Cleeves, who were original New Plymouth settlers, had
been merchants in Devon.

Massachusetts was largely colonised from Devonshire. In 1622 over
80 citizens of the town left for the New World.

The city endured one of the worst sieges of the Civil War, and was the only place in the entire West Country to remain loyal to Parliament.

For the last 200 years, of course, Plymouth, and Dartmouth nearby, have been the site of the Royal Arsenal and Naval Dockyards and the prosperity of the city during the last century has depended on this.

During the last war, Plymouth was gutted by air raids, and I remember driving through the centre the following morning not knowing whether I was on a road or driving over the remains of a house.

It is because Plymouth's history has been so violent that so little of it is visible. It has endured sieges, fires and air raids. It has had to rebuild itself time and time again. And consequently the city you see, at least in the centre, will disappoint you: it could remind you more of Dallas than of Devonshire. Only around the Hoe can you see a few old houses and cobbled pavements.

You may notice that though this city has been rebuilt it still lacks either a theatre or an Opera House. Several attempts have been made in the last few years to get these necessities built, but the Socialist City Council has always refused.

SEVEN

Cornwall:
A Few Facts and Fallacies

A tiny part of the boundary between Devon and Cornwall runs through my farm. Therefore I can be said to have a small foot in either county. I repeat this to show that I am impartial. But you will notice that I have devoted more of my space in this book and of your time on this journey to Devonshire than to Cornwall. This is because Devonshire is very much larger than Cornwall.

Cornwall does not regard itself as just another county in England. The true Cornishman still looks upon the rest of the country as foreign land. I have heard many Cornishmen say that they are going 'up to England'. They refer to Cornwall as the 'Duchy'. They are insular and they have every right to be so, because this Cornish peninsula is almost an island, with the river Tamar as its eastern boundary, the Channel to the south and the Atlantic to the north.

Cornwall is as distinct from Devon as Portugal is from Spain. It is extremely hard to put your finger on what that difference is. It is only partially due to the scenery. Even motoring casually through the Duchy, you become aware imperceptibly of an historical dimension, and of a past which is strange and new to you. You get the sense of being on foreign soil.

F. E. Halliday, in his excellent history of Cornwall, makes a vivid image which is unforgettable.

'If you take the three-hundred-mile journey from London to Land's End,' he says, 'we travel also in time, back towards our beginning, *at an average rate of a million years for every mile of the journey'*. Cornwall is that much older than the rest of the country. In the beginning the Duchy lay under a tropical sea. Then, after the convulsion that threw up Snowdon and the Scottish Highlands some 300 million years ago, the Devonian sandstones began to be laid down under the oceans that covered western Europe. At this time, the mountains of Scotland must have been as high as the Himalayas. Gradually the rock eroded, the debris settled at the bottom of the sea.

Halliday estimates that for 'fifty million years limestone was deposited in the shallow waters that lapped the east coast of Cornwall'. Then came another convulsion, when the rocks of Cornwall and Devon were violently folded in the Armorican mountains almost as high as the Alps are today. The fiery matter that lay beneath the oldest sedimentary rocks thrust itself into the folds, where it solidified as granite, while gases and boiling liquids forced their way through fissures in the heat-transformed rocks and hardened aureoles left the granite domes to form metallic veins.

Geologically speaking, Cornwall has had two existences. That is to say, it had existed for 100 million years or so before being covered again by a shallow tropical sea which drowned the mammals that had evolved upon it. Then gradually the sea retreated, the lowlands emerged forming the coastal plain linking the mountain range which is now Bodmin Moor with those mountains further west. A tropical sea already existed between the Isles of Scilly and Land's End. Bodmin is all that remains of the great Armorican mountains which were thrown up at the first cataclysm.

Cornwall is a unique place in which to study geology. Some might say that the rocks beneath the land there are more interesting than anything on it.

The geological significance of the county, however, will not be the reason why you sense that you are in a place with an ancient history. Nor will you get that from the buildings which you see around you: for the most part they are of the last century. How, then, do we explain this overwhelming sense of the past which everyone feels in Cornwall? It is, I think, due to such things as Trethevy Quoit on the southern edge of Bodmin. I think this Quoit is the most beautiful thing in the

22 *St. Ives: the modesty of little boat*

whole of Cornwall, and certainly the most impressive, in its savage and uncompromising dimensions. You may go to such places as Tintagel and get a feeling of medievalism which, by being remote, appears romantic. But ruined castles cannot present you with a new experience; Trethevy Quoit can do this. It represents a past which we cannot romanticise about because we can hardly imagine what it was like at all.

As soon as you get to Bodmin I want you to head direct to Trethevy Quoit, ignoring towns and so-called beauty spots on the way; because once you have seen these stones you will have a perspective, something with which to measure the trivial, the transient and the trashy.

It is impossible to give even a brief outline of the history of Cornwall here: I recommend Halliday's *History of Cornwall* published by Duckworth in 1959, and I urge you to read this book before you visit the Duchy. Some people, of course, think that the past is irrelevant and that concern with it is unrealistic and an escape; but such a point of view is stupid. History is our own diary. Everything we are and everything that we have inherited is part of the historical process. If you think that the Stone Age or the Bronze Age is something too remote to concern you, consider what sort of life you would be living if it were not for what you have inherited from the past. I have often thought, as I lugged a sack of barley meal across my farmyard, how many thousands of such burdens I would have to carry before I myself came to invent the wheel or the wheelbarrow. The answer is probably much longer than we are now removed from Palaeolithic man. And how many thousands of buckets of water would you have to carry from the well before your creative faculties produced the pump? Everything that we use and take for granted has come to us from the past. If it were not for the struggle of the Stone Age man, where would we be ourselves? The answer, of course, is we would be in the Stone Age too. It you can see history as the process in your *own* development, a sort of personal diary, then it springs to life. You will find when you invented this, when you saved yourself the trouble of doing that, the past is always present.

The first invasion of Cornwall occurred around 2,000 B.C., when explorers from the Aegean sailed west in search of copper and tin. These people probably sailed across the Bay of Biscay in nothing more

3 Perranporth Beach

than a coracle. That they settled in Cornwall is evidenced by their large tombs, such as that at Pawton near Wadebridge. Some time after these people, another set of immigrants landed in Cornwall, probably from Brittany; evidence of their settlements can be seen from the small barrows.

After the Stone Age, the so-called Beaker Folk reached Cornwall and made settlements which can still be seen at Callington and another near Lanivet.

Cornwall at this time was more civilised than the rest of England. The reason seems to be that because of its geographical position it was the overland route between Brittany and Ireland, and Brittany and Wales. Gold used to be mined in both Ireland and Wales, and of course Cornwall had its own tin and copper mines which brought influences to its shores from as far away as the Mediterranean. The merchants at this time used to go up the Camel estuary by way of Padstow, Wadebridge, Bodmin and the River Fowey. Gold ornaments precisely similar to those found in Ireland have been unearthed on this route. But trade with the Continent declined rapidly after the Roman Conquest of Britain; once the Empire had been established here merchants came to England across the Channel. Cornwall became cut off from its Continental influences; whereas the county had been ahead of the rest of the country before the Romans, it now lagged very much behind, after the first century.

Many visitors to Cornwall think of it as the County of the Druids. They believe that every ruin they see belonged to this ancient priesthood. This is not the case.

According to Julius Caesar the Druids were a priestly aristocracy, entry to which was obtained only by a vigorous novitiate. Some reports state that a novice had to stand naked in a mountain stream during the night and compose a poem of 500 lines in a strict metre which he had to recite at dawn. Whatever truth there is in this, it seems that the priesthood was difficult to enter. Caesar comments on the Druids' tendency to make sacrifices:

> They are much given to superstition and those who are involved in wars either make human sacrifices or vow that they will do so, and use the Druids as their

agents at these ceremonies, for they think that the Divine Power cannot be con-
sulted unless a human life is paid for by a human life . . . some tribes make great
images whose limbs, woven of wickerwork, they cram with live human victims
and then place fire below and slay them by the flames . . . when the supply of
victims failed they have been known to lay hands on wholly innocent persons.

Caesar states that Druidism originated in Britain. Very little indeed is
known about the cult. It is not true that the stone relics found on
Bodmin are anything to do with the Druids. The Druids left no sacri-
ficial stones or evidence of their religious rites beyond two or three
circles of stones similar to Stonehenge. Many of their beliefs, such as
the benefit of passing children through a stone hole to cure certain
illnesses, and the fire festivals, which are still celebrated in Cornwall,
linger on today.

Up to the sixteenth century Cornwall had its own language. It was not
until 1540 that the Creed and Lord's Prayer were first taught in
English. The historian Norden, writing in 1580, says: 'Of late the
Cornishmen have much conformed themselves to the use of the
English tongue and their English is equal to the best, especially in
the eastern parts.' It was, of course, the Reformation that brought in
the English Liturgy and Bible. The Cornish justifiably rebelled. In 1549
they said; 'we will have our own service; we refuse this new English.'
The language lingered in isolated places around Land's End until the
end of the eighteenth century, but none is spoken today. Apart from
an esoteric society which is vainly attempting to revive the language
and produces an occasional magazine in Cornish, none is written.
This is a pity, because when the Cornish lost their language they
began to lose their cultural identity as well. The same, of course,
can be said of their economic independence: this was taken from
them when the Mint at Truro was closed, and the Cornish were denied
access to their own credit. 'Give me control of the currency', Nathan
Rothschild said for all bankers, 'and I do not care a damn who rules the
country.'
    London had no need to raise an army to subjugate Cornwall; it
merely had to close the Mint. Cornish currency had been backed by

tin. This closure of the Truro Mint tethered the Duchy to Lombard Street.

The only sign you will see today of the Cornish language is, of course, in the place-names. The old line is:

> By *tre*, *pol* and *pen*
> You shall know the Cornishman.

Tre means a ship: *pen* means headland: *car* is the same as the Latin *castra*. The Cornish word *parc* meaning a field can be found in parts of Devon which border Cornwall. I have several fields on my own farm which are known as parcs. *Bow*, *bed* or *bos* mean a dwelling; *lis* a Court or palace: *hel* a river. A mine was *wheal* and *col* a hill. These prefixes are still extant. I have heard Cornish spoken and could not distinguish it from Welsh. Here is the Lord's Prayer in Cornish:

> *Agan Tâs, nêb ûs yn nêf, bydhens uchdfys dhe*
> *hanow, dêns dhe wlascor, dhe vôdh re by gwryes*
> *yn nor cepar hag yn nef. Ro dhynny hydhew agan*
> *pûb dydh bara. Ha gâf dhynny agan cammow,*
> *kepar del gevyn ny nêb ûs ow cammé er agan pyn*
> *ny. Ha na dôg ny yn antel, mês gwyth ny dheworth*
> *drôc. Yn delna re bo.*

But it would be a waste of time to learn Cornish: there is practically no Cornish literature except one or two miracle plays, a sacred poem or two, and a few fables.

These Cornish miracle plays compare favourably with those of York, Coventry and Chester. They are called *The Origin of the World*, *The Passion of Our Lord*, and *The Resurrection* and make up the cycle known as *Ordinalia*. I have been unable to see a performance of any one of these plays, but Halliday quotes a passage of undoubted literary merit dealing with the lyrical attachment between David and Bathsheba;

> *Damsel, er dha, jentylys,*
> *dysqua dhym a th kerensa . . .*
> *Lady, in thy gentleness,*
> *I beseech thee, love me;*
> *Never have I seen a woman*
> *Pleases me above thee;*

140

24 A *China Clay pyramid near St. Auste*

Thou shalt have my palaces,
All my halls and chambers,
Be my love and live with me,
And I thy lover ever.

The Cornish lodes, or mineral veins in the granite, were worked for both copper and tin thousands of years before any coal was mined in England. Indeed the history of Cornish tin-mining goes back long before the Roman Conquest, almost to the Bronze Age.

There are two stories told of how tin was discovered in Cornwall.

The first is that St Piran, an Irish saint, came over on a mission to convert the Celts, bearing with him a bottle of Irish whiskey. As he landed from his coracle he was met by a Cornish hermit called Chigwidden. Apparently the saint's spirit helped to convert the hermit, and they drank the entire bottle.

'Bedad', said St Piran, 'bothered if there be another drop to be squeezed out! Never mind, my spiritual brother: I'll show you how to distil the crayture. Pile me up some stones, and we'll get up the divil of a fire, and we shall manage to make enough to expel the deuce out of ould Cornwall.'

So the hermit collected a number of black stones together to make an oven and they built a roaring fire, whereupon a stream of liquid silver ran from the stones and tin was discovered.

The story is certainly untrue, for tin was probably discovered nearly 1,000 years before the saint was born. The other story is reported by S. Baring-Gould in his *Book of the West*. It is one which I have often heard referred to in Cornwall, and is to the effect that Joseph of Arimathea came in a boat to Cornwall, bringing the child Jesus with him, and the latter taught him how to extract tin and purge it of wolfram. The basis of this myth is probably that under the Angevin kings of France, who ruled England after the Norman Conquest, the Jews leased the Cornish mineral rights. Even recently when tin was flashed—that is, revealed in the lode—the tinner would shout 'Joseph was in the tin trade', which is probably a corruption of 'St Joseph to the tinner's aid'.

However, the connection between the Jews and the Cornish tin

25 Typical ruin of Cornish tin mine

mines can be traced in many places in Cornwall today. The old smelting-houses are still called Jew's Houses, and many inhabitants of the stannary towns of Helston, Truro, Lostwithiel and Liskeard still bear Jewish names; perhaps the name of Port Isaac also derives from this association. On the other hand, it is possible that many of the Jewish names and words in the county come from no more than the people's habit of choosing patronyms from the Old Testament.

How old the tin industry is can be gauged from the following quotation from Diodorus Siculus, who wrote in the time of the Emperor Augustus of Rome:

> The inhabitants of that extremity of Britain which is called Belerion both excel in hospitality and also, by reason of their intercourse with foreign merchants, are civilised in their mode of life. These prepare the tin, working very skilfully the earth which produces it. The ground is rocky, but it has in it earthy veins, the produce of which is brought down and melted and purified. Then, when they have cast it into the form of cubes, they carry it to a certain island adjoining Britain, called Ictis. During the recess of the tide, the intervening space is left dry, and they carry over abundance of tin in carts . . . From thence the traders who purchase the tin of the natives transport it to Gaul, and finally, travelling through Gaul on foot, in about 30 days bring their burdens on horses to the mouth of the Rhine.

Ictis was in all probability St Michael's Mount.

Little archaeological evidence remains that the Romans worked the tin mines. But since they used our native lead in the baths they built at Bath, it is also likely that they made use of the Cornish tin.

The Saxon invasion then destroyed the industry, and this was followed by the Danish freebooters, who sailed up the Cornish rivers when they also burnt the Devon stannary towns of Tavistock and Lydford in 997.

The Normans revived the industry and Cornish tin and copper was distributed by Italian merchants across Europe as far as the Levant. At Florence an old record refers to Cornish tin being smelted at Venice and being stamped with the Lion of St Mark.

Not for nothing was Cornwall kept as a Royal Duchy, for it was the most prosperous of English counties. Queen Elizabeth fostered her revenues by introducing German engineers and workmen, who improved the machinery at the mines. She also appointed Sir Walter Raleigh, Lord Warden of the Stannaries in 1601.

At this period the tin industry had established its own Stannary Parliament, and what is more important the Cornish, with their minerals as backing, were enabled to issue their own currency, which was minted by the Bishop of Truro, up till the time when Britain's coinage was centralised in 1838. As in Devon, the Stannary towns also had their own Stannary Courts, which meant that ordinary Justices of the Peace had no jurisdiction over mining disputes.

The mining industry all over the world owes a debt to Cornwall. It was in Cornwall that the modern technique of mining was developed with the introduction of deep shafts, pumps and steam haulage engines. Some of this equipment is still exported to mines in other parts of the world which are now more prosperous than those in Cornwall itself. A man called Trevithick was experimenting with locomotives as early as 1797. In 1801 his full-scale Puffing Devil was given a trial on the road between Camborne and Tehidy. Subsequently an engine to his design was placed on tracks and in 1808 ran on rails at Euston till one of the rails broke and the engine overturned. Trevithick was the inventor of the steam engine, and George Stephenson, who has been given the credit, developed his invention.

You will not be many hours in Cornwall before you become conscious of King Arthur. He is both ubiquitous and mysterious. You can neither avoid him nor reach him.

The first mention of Arthur is in the Historia Britonum dated about 685, in which Nennius says: 'The Saxons increased in numbers in Britain until they were checked, not, however, by Ambrosius or Aurelianus but by one Arthur who used to fight against them in company with the Kings of the Britons.' Arthur himself was not a king but a general. It is known that he defeated the Saxons in several battles, the last being at Badon Hill. On that day the legend reports: '960 men fell before the assault of Arthur and no one felled them save he alone.' After this imaginative beginning, Geoffrey of Monmouth indulged in his script-writing technique and cast Arthur as 'the son of Igerna and Pendragon, King of Britain. After defeating the Saxons,

Picts and Scots, he added Ireland, Iceland and the Orkneys to his domain, then subdued Norway, Acquitaine and Gaul before waging a successful war against the Romans'. For his finale Geoffrey of Monmouth makes his hero decapitate a Spanish giant on the top of St Michael's Mount.

This fairy tale does not bear any historical examination. But Cornwall does contain innumerable references to Arthur which cannot be ignored. Camelford was, of course, the original Camelot. Arthur's Hall still exists on Bodmin; Tintagel was the site of King Arthur's castle with Merlin's cave beneath; Kelly Rounds is another of his seats. There is also a Merlin's Rock in Mousehole and at Sennen, the place at which Arthur dined after being summoned to repel an invasion. Two of the islands in the Scilly group are known as Great and Little Arthur.

By the middle of the nineteenth century the Cornish mining industry ran into disaster. Production of copper fell from 160,000 tons in 1865 to less than 500 tons by the end of the century. Tin had been discovered in Malaya and Bolivia, copper in the United States and Rhodesia. The Cornish miners were half-starved. One of them left an account of his suffering:

> My father had the standard wages for service hands which was £2.5.0 a month and I was earning 10/- a month so that £2.15.0 a month had to provide for five of us. For our breakfast we had barley gruel which constituted about three-quarters of water and ½d. worth of skim milk thickened with barley flour, a concoction which went by the name of 'sky blue and sinker'. We lived about half a mile from the mine and I had to come home to dinner. I was sometimes so feeble that I could scarcely crawl along. For dinner we had a barley pastie with two bits of pork on potatoes and for supper a barley cake, or potatoes or turnips with a barley cover. Everything was very dear; groceries such as raisins and currants were 10d. a pound, tea 4/- a pound, and the common brown sugar 5d. a pound. I never saw at that time such a thing as jam.

Many of the Cornish miners emigrated. It was they who opened up the mines in Peru, participating in the gold rush in California, and discovering the Australian gold mines. The population of the county fell precipitately. But at this period the china clay industry brought some prosperity to the county, and the railways began to bring the Duchy more in touch with the rest of the country.

But even in this depression of the last century Cornwall had more cultural life than it has today. At Truro there was a Philosophical Society, and many literary, scientific and musical Institutes. The one industry which was stable was fishing; especially for pilchards which, centred at St Ives, supplied a Mediterranean market and exported a great part of its catch to Italy.

But by the beginning of this century, the fishing industry had declined, unable to compete with the deep-sea trawlers coming from France and East Anglia which poached the grounds. And for some inexplicable reason, the shoals of pilchards disappeared. In the 1920s Cornwall began to see that its future lay in exploiting its scenery and climate. The term *Cornish Riviera* was coined. The 'Penzance Express' was started. Various artists' colonies were established in St Ives, Mevagissey and Port Isaac. The county which had led the way in industrialisation, both with mining and ironworks, now found itself dependent on its quaint little coombes. Greedy for some kind of prosperity, it failed to plan the invasion or to realise that within a generation its incredibly beautiful coastline could be spoiled. What it has done is to trade a heritage for a brief relief from its difficulties.

Although some of the tin mines are now working again, and clay pits are still thriving, the county's future is extremely precarious. The land is not suitable for large-scale mechanical farming and the smallholder growing early vegetables or flowers finds he cannot compete with the produce which is flown in to Covent Garden from Malta and France. Consequently, Cornishmen continue to leave Cornwall and people moving into the county are those who have found their livelihood elsewhere and settle there only in retirement. The county is without a university.

EIGHT

South Cornwall

One of the things you will notice in Mevagissey and the other towns in Cornwall is the large number of small pubs. They seem more numerous than anywhere else in the country. Perhaps this is partially due to the mining; or perhaps it is a relic of their independence. Even so, though there are a great number of inns in Cornwall still, there were once very many more. In some streets of Redruth and Camelford every house was once a beer house. This may seem strange today. We should remember that the licensing laws were not introduced even in England until 1861. Previous to that, a house could sell liquor so long as it paid the excise. It is extraordinary how many liberties we have lost: the Cornish used to brew their beer, were free to sell it and buy it with money that was also home made.

But before the nineteenth century, Cornish inns had as bad a reputation as Cornish roads.

You ended your tour of Devon at Plymouth. I have divided Cornwall into three sections: South Cornwall, Bodmin and North Cornwall. And from Plymouth you will be well placed to tour the first section.

I would like you to make an early start because I want you to reach Truro for lunch: today you need not rely on your picnic basket. Instead telephone the 'Rendez-vous de Gourmet' to secure a table.

Having crossed the Tamar into the Duchy I suggest you take the coast road to Crafthale, Downderry and Looe.

Looe is a genuine Cornish fishing village and existed in the reign of Edward I. You will notice the hydrangeas and geraniums flowering out of doors and that many of the houses have staircases on the outside walls, presumably as a precaution against flooding. The pilchard-fishing from Looe has almost stopped, but during the summer it is possible to go out shark-fishing. Granite is still shipped down the canal, but the copper is no longer mined. Geologists have found fossilised trees beneath the shore and regard a place called Millendreath just outside Looe as being of considerable interest.

After Looe follow the road to Polperro and to Fowey. Fowey is still very beautiful, and was a seaport at the time of the Crusades, sending many ships to the Holy Land. Later, in the Elizabethan era, it gave its name to the Fowey Gallants, the seamen who used to plunder the coast of Normandy and created such havoc there that the French had to fit out an expedition against the town. There are still some very old houses in it, including several of the fourteenth century. The north aisle of the church is said to date from 1336. In the south aisle is a monument to John Treffrey, who was a well-known eccentric at the end of the last century. He built his own monument in the church, and had his own grave dug before he died, then lay in it and swore up at the sexton to show that he had no fear of damnation.

There are many mines—copper, tin, kaolin—in the area. These china clay deposits are still flourishing.

At Fowey you will find a ferry. There is no way of bypassing St Austell but after the town you can take the coast road again via Porthpear to Mevagissey.

When you leave Mevagissey take the side road to St Ewe, Polnassich, then head across country to Creed, ignoring the 'B' road which you will cross. From Creed it is only a dozen signposts on to Probus and I particularly want you to go there.

For after Crediton the village of Probus contains what I think is one of the most beautiful churches in the two counties. It was at one time attached to a Priory which was founded by King Athelstan about A.D. 930, and was rebuilt by the Normans. Apart from the piscina in the sanctuary, none of this period remains. The tower is the real glory of the church and is an architectural masterpiece. The church is built of Cornish granite and the proportions are outstanding.

Between Probus and Truro you will pass many ill-proportioned

26 *Cornish road walls partially built from*
Celtic ruins

modern houses and you may wonder what has happened to the skill and craftsmanship which went into the building of St Probus. But they have not all disappeared; it is rather that this age has failed to provide a vehicle for the skills which are still there in the hand. For instance, if you glance at the new bypass outside Truro you will notice that where the road has been widened and where the Council has erected a new wall along the grass verge, it has not constructed it of concrete blocks or posts and barbed wire, but built a wall in the traditional style of the area, used from time immemorial. The method is to take small granite or slate slabs then put the stones of one layer leaning at one angle, another leaning in the opposite direction and so on. This produces a herringbone effect. No mortar is used between the stones: they are chipped to fit. Such walls stand for centuries. Sometimes the top is turfed. In Devon it is possible to tell exactly where you are by noticing the type of wall adjoining the road. Another sign that the skills which used to belong to the craftsman are still in existence when a use can be found for them can be seen on the thatched roofs. The roof of the 'Wheel Inn' on the way to Truro is a fine example. The thatcher has patterned the roof with an emblem of a cartwheel. Only somebody who has tried to thatch even a hayrick himself can assess the degree of skill that must have been required on that roof. But if these skills were used in the construction of Truro Cathedral they were to little effect. The fine proportions which are so noticeable at the church of St Probus are entirely missing from this early twentieth-century edifice. Looking at it one realises that a Cathedral is not made of stone alone.

Truro was made a city in 1877, when the see of Cornwall was separated from Devonshire. But the original importance of Truro was that it was here that the Cornish coinage was minted and a Coinage Hall still stands. A monument in the Cathedral dated 1636 records the adventures of Owen Fitzpen, who captured an Algerian ship on which he was a slave and carried it into Cartagena where he sold it for £600 and settled in Truro with the money.

There are also some splendid terraces of Regency houses in the town, and some late Georgian houses.

Truro is worth a visit because it is an oasis in the culinary desert

27 *Truro Cathedral from North East*

of Cornwall. By some extraordinary freak it has the 'Rendez-vous de Gourmet', which is one of the few three-star restaurants in England, and is not only good but cheap.

If you are in Cornwall at the right time of the year you can now head from Truro to the Helford River, which has a splendid array of oyster-beds. Or if oysters are out of season, cut across country, avoiding Helston if you can, and make for Newlyn, which is on the outskirts of Penzance. Here you will find a whole street of warehouses full of crustaceans. You can buy fresh crabs weighing four to five pounds each, a basket full of lobsters and even a crayfish, all costing under £1. Adjoining the warehouses there is a fascinating seaman's shop festooned with nylon nets, coloured sou'westers and all the gear that the small fishing ports of Newlyn and Mousehole use. Time spent in small fishing villages like these is more rewarding than if spent in Penzance.

Like every town in Cornwall, Penzance was founded by a saint: in this instance by St Antony. 'Pensans' in Cornish means 'Saint's Headland'.

It is possible that you may notice a statue in the town of Sicilian marble within an Ionic portico celebrating Sir Humphry Davy, philosopher and chemist, who also invented the miner's safety-lamp, and was born in 1778 in a house which stood where the statue now stands. You may come across one or two old pubs in the side streets, but these have been spoilt by being made self-conscious: brass capstans used for tables; portholes for spittoons; and other pieces of interior decoration inspired by a jackdaw.

In 1595 Penzance was raided in force by the Spaniards, who landed at Mousehole and destroyed the village. In 1646 the town was sacked by Cromwell's forces.

One tradition from its past is still observed on 28 June; the 'Eves of St John and St Peter' are celebrated by the burning of tar barrels erected on the quay. Similar bonfires are lighted at other towns along the coast. After torches have been lit from the bonfire, the ancient game of 'Thread the Needle' starts in the streets.

Boys and girls join hands and run through the town crying 'An eye! An eye! An eye!' At length they stop and the last couple raise their hands to form an eye through which the rest of the crowd, in the shape of a needle, thread. A similar custom persists in Germany and Norway, and it is thought that the origin is in the celebration of the sun festivals.

From Penzance you can either take a plane or a boat to the Scilly Isles. The Scilly Isles, once called the Fortunate Isles, were settled in about 1700 B.C. by immigrants from Brittany. At that time they were probably 40 or more feet higher than they are today. The considerable subsidence that occurred on these islands may account for the legend of Lyonesse, the country from which Tristan derived, or perhaps it may account for the legend of Avalon, the mysterious island to which Arthur was conveyed by Queens when he was mortally wounded in his last battle.

The Scilly Isles were, it must be assumed, a kind of *Laguna Morte* for the mainland because there are on the islands so many ancient tombs. It is doubtful whether the islands have ever supported a large population themselves; it is probable that the dead were ferried over from the mainland to be buried there. However, another explanation has been given which cannot be proved or disproved. There are many walls on the islands which disappear into the sea, proving there was once a considerable subsidence. There is a legend that Avalon was joined to the islands, and it disappeared like Atlantis.

The islanders' chief occupation is the growing of early daffodils and tomatoes. An aeroplane service now ferries the tourists there; consequently the islands are becoming less dependent on horticulture. Like so many places in Cornwall, the Scilly Isles were once graveyards for shipping, but radar has lessened this hazard. A few hulks of wrecks can be seen at low water.

Against your inclinations I would advise you not to go round the Land's End peninsula. This foot of Cornwall has been lamed by caravans. I suggest you bypass it and drive across to St Ives, which has a splendid bay. Camborne and Redruth grew up as mining towns: they are unattractive. From St Ives it is expedient to leave the main road and take the coast road to St Agnes.

Why is it that Cornwall has apparently suffered more from tourism than Devonshire? The answer is that Cornwall is not one-fifth of the size of Devonshire, and in proportion has a very much larger coastline.

I knew it when I was a child before so much of this coast had been turned into a car park. I can remember the fishing villages when the fishermen *were* fishermen, and consequently I am indignant at what I see now. The Council for the Preservation of Rural England and the National Trust are supposed to do something to preserve our inheritance. It is obviously too late to prevent the desecration that has occurred. Clearly unless the whole of the Cornish coast is to be entirely raided by vandals, some new legislation is required. It would have to have powers to destroy some of these excrescences that have been allowed to appear in the last 30 years. I am thinking particularly of the nauseating little structures which call themselves bungalows and are built beside many Cornish monuments. There is no other nation in the entire world that would allow that kind of thing to occur. It is as if the Egyptians used the Sphinx for the foundation of a block of flats. We went to Egypt to unearth Tutankhamen, and are now worrying about the tombs that are going to be flooded by the Aswan High Dam. I suspect it is time we turned some of our attention to our own shores. Shall we have to wait till the Egyptians come here to clean *us* up?

28 *Delabole Quarry : the navel of Cornwall*

NINE

Bodmin

I now want you to head straight from the coast to Bodmin. And by Bodmin I mean Trethevy Quoit and not the town on the edge of the moor. It will not disappoint you.

This grave consists of four great pieces of uncarved granite placed at angles supporting a fifth slab placed above them at an angle. Each plane and surface appeals to the eye. Epstein and Brancusi would have made a pilgrimage to it. I came across it by accident, and my present interest in Cornish history is because I want to understand how these beautiful stones got into this position 4,000 years ago. I believe they will serve as a similar introduction to other people.

The Quoit was probably built by the peoples who invaded this country about 2,000 B.C., who derived from the Aegean and settled in France, Spain, Portugal and Cornwall in search of metals out of which to make bronze. We know that their method of burying their dead was to erect great slabs of rock to form a mausoleum, over which they placed mounds of earth. They came to Cornwall almost certainly for tin. There is every evidence that it was mined as long ago as that. These Eastern people worshipped an Earth Goddess and practised communal burial. The soil above the Quoit was, of course, washed off by the rain and the structure revealed, as it stands today. You may wonder how these primitive architects erected such slabs of granite when each one weighs 100 tons or more. Halliday suggests that:

> A deep rectangular trench was dug, then five great slabs of granite, some 12 feet high and five feet wide, were hauled into position on wooden rollers where they were raised with levers and rawhide ropes until their bases sank into the trench to

Trethevy Quoit : B.C. 1800

form three walls of a chamber. This was then sealed by another stone set back from the entrance, so forming an open antechamber or forecourt, though a gap was left at one of the bottom corners of the sealing stone, big enough for a man to crawl through. Finally, an earthen ramp was built against the back of the chamber, and up this the gangs of straining men inched the massive capstone, or quoit, until it covered the tomb.

Many historians have suggested that Trethevy Quoit and similar monuments such as the Hurlers, which you will see dotted around Bodmin, were Druids' altars. This is nonsense. They pre-date the Druids by several thousand years. You will think it strange that a people who could build such indestructible monuments as the quoits at Chun, Mulfra and Zennor should have been unable to leave two stones together to indicate how they lived. It seems that whatever this civilisation was, it was based on a belief in immortality: that is to say, like the Egyptians, they made their tombs more durable than their houses. When one comes to think of it, I suppose the same standards operate today, though perhaps not to this degree. We do know that belief in an after-life was so strong amongst the peoples of this peninsula that the Druid priests would lend money on the understanding that they would be repaid after they were dead.

Bodmin Moor is not so impressive scenically as Dartmoor or Exmoor, but it has a quality of its own. The most casual visitor will feel that his nose is suddenly rubbed in the past. The past is of granite. The moor is littered with prehistoric monuments. They are not all Christian nor are they all Druidic. Many of the crosses have been placed on sites which were hallowed by pagan cults. The form of the cross most prevalent in Cornwall is a shaft surmounted by a round head from which a Greek cross stands in relief. Some of the crosses are ornamented either with scroll-work or with some symbolic device, as is the cross in St Columb churchyard which bears the trefoil, a well-known symbol of the Holy Trinity. You may notice several with the fleur-de-lis carved on them as at Washaway near Bodmin. This is nothing to do with France, but the fleur-de-lis was used as a symbol for the Virgin Mary. Many of these crosses and monuments can still be seen. How many have been removed to be used as gate-posts or lintels is another matter. On one drive across Bodmin I myself counted seven crosses which had been built into walls to strengthen them. An even greater number, of course, have been broken up to be used as foundations for roads. Even so, there are still many primitive monuments which should be seen. The cross at Perranzabuloe, nine feet high, was not designed by Barbara Hepworth or Henry Moore.

And you will also see several cartwheel crosses at Trevillet. There is one used as a post for a garden gate at Lanherne; there is another cross with a Saxon inscription on the base and a Child Christ figure set against a cartwheel crucifix. Many of these crosses have been erected over holy wells. There are innumerable wells in Cornwall, the waters of which are supposed to cure some particular ailment: generally a small chapel was built over the spring, as at St Cleer. It used to be the custom at these wells to leave part of one's clothing as an offering to the spirit or patron saint. Sometimes these rags were hung on the gorse growing round the well. The idea derives from the notion that the ailment or disease remains where the clothing is left. A precisely similar superstition is still held in India. Some of these wells, like the one at Roche, with a simple archway over it, are extremely beautiful. Here the locals used to throw pins into the water to obtain a blessing.

But it is not the Christian relics which are so awe-inspiring as the cromlechs such as the Lanyon cromlech at Madron, or the slabs of granite at Zennor. Several of these cromlechs or quoits have been knocked down, as at St Columb Major. You will be fascinated by the holed stones at Anguidal Down, Madron, where the centre stone is four feet in diameter and one foot thick, with a hole one foot three inches in diameter through it. This holed stone is probably of Druidic origin, as of course is the circle at Boscawen. It consists of 19 stones and is about 73 feet in diameter. The one stone set at an angle gives you a suggestion that the whole may have been some kind of sundial. This is not impossible.

At Kingbear the land is still strewn with granite but you can see the great china clay heaps breaking the horizon. Most people say that they disfigure the landscape. But I feel that they are too monumental to do that. Indeed they have become the landscape. Cornish china clay was discovered in the middle of the eighteenth century and has been mined ever since. It is not used merely for pottery. Its uses are innumerable;

as kaolin in medicinal preparations; for the manufacture of paper; rubber, including motor-tyres; for the dressing of fabrics, especially linen; and more recently the industry has become even more prosperous since the clay is used for the manufacture of heat-resistant crucibles and certain equipment employed in nuclear fission.

Launceston is a typical Cornish market town, with a mud-pie overlooking it. This is the remains of the Norman castle, which was a stronghold in the Civil War, and finally became derelict in the seventeenth century.

In the Market Square you cannot fail to notice the 'White Hart Hotel' which was one of the great coaching inns of the West Country. The main lounge with a glass roof was once an open courtyard. Around this lounge you can still see playbills dating from the time when the dining room was the town theatre. These are dated 1772. I do not suppose Launceston has seen a play since then. The main doorway of the hotel is a magnificent arch which was taken either from the old Norman Priory or from the castle.

It is now a Trust House. I visited it in 1965, unknowingly and uncaringly, in the poet Southey's footsteps. Cream was not served with the tea, toast and honey were unobtainable, and the cakes were covered in a kind of garnish of wax festooned with little silver ball-bearings.

St Mary Magdalene, the Parish Church of Launceston, is one of the most impressive in Cornwall. Its heavily carved exterior is unique. It is a pity that this fine building should be crowded by adjacent shops. A church of this distinction needs to be seen in perspective. But St Mary Magdalene has a car park within five yards of the porch. Inside the church the carved bench ends are particularly interesting, especially those which depict animals, such as a heron catching trout and a lion in play.

There is a beautiful church clock on the tower. Apparently the tower on which this clock stands has occasionally been used for some strange purposes. A letter exists in which a shocked commercial traveller complains to the Bishop of Exeter;

> My Lord,—I should think myself guilty of neglect were I to refrain from making the following circumstances publicly known.
> On Saturday last I rode from Stratton to Launceston, and on passing the Church

at the latter place I saw several persons weighing a bullock in the belfrey of the tower, and others standing ready to weigh some pigs.

I stopped and enquired whether it was usual to weigh bullocks and pigs in the belfry. One of the persons replied in the affirmative; upon which I asked 'Is your Church then a shambles?' The man smiled and muttered something I did not comprehend.

Now, my Lord, it appears to me a great shame that this consecrated place should be so defiled every market day. If the clergyman of Launceston, who is, I understand, a pleasurable man and fond of the sports of the field and good cheer, connives at the pollution, I hope you will interfere to put a stop to it, now you are brought acquainted with the fact.

I am, my Lord, etc., John Wright, a commercial traveller, Launceston, Nov. 23rd, 1831.

Please note that I wrote on the subject to the Rev. J. Rowe, Nov. 23rd.

But if you want to find the centre of vitality in a town like Launceston, do not go to the church, which is empty, the castle, which is derelict, or the inn, which has the air of a commercial travellers' rendezvous. You go, I think, to the Market where you can still see farmers' wives sitting in front of their baskets of shallots, honey, cream, and little bunches of primroses or daffodils, or you wander into the ironmonger's and stare at the fascinating shiny tools.

TEN

North Cornwall

After leaving Bodmin Moor I suggest you drive to the coast at Padstow. Padstow's virtue was that it was a fishing town with all the fascination and delicious smells that go with it. Unhappily the small boats and nets attracted so many visitors to the Quay that the fishermen were able to abandon them and now do little more than take the visitors out in the bay.

From Padstow I suggest that you drive to Delabole. Quarries are not generally thought of as beauty spots, but this is one of the most fascinating views in Cornwall. Here is a quarry which has been mining the famous Delabole slate for over 1,000 years. The deeper they go into the earth the darker and more beautiful the slate is. As you stand on the edge of the quarry you wonder how many millions of years it was since this slate was formed in some fold of the earth's crust, and what sort of pressure was then put upon the clay. Evidence of the cataclysm that occurred probably 100 million years ago can be held in your hand: pieces of slate bearing a fossil of a fern leaf, a snake or a mouse. Delabole slate is not reckoned as a precious material, but it looks it. Lumps weighing anything up to ten tons emerge and are sawn by hand, then smoothed. These splendid slabs of slate are now used for facing University and Government offices, whereas they were once only valued for dairy floors because they keep a room cool. These smooth, almost black pieces of slate are extremely beautiful. The quarrymen will let you take a piece away, and think you are silly to want to do so. But this slate is worth having—to feel its smoothness against your cheek or use as a paperweight. There is no inscription on a slab of Delabole. It bears no silly rhyme or motto, or any mark of this or any other age. It is what it is, and in its primeval remoteness it makes a comment on what we are.

It is worth going to this quarry to observe the workmen cutting and polishing these slabs of slate. They seem to love every block of it, and are as proud of its planes and surfaces as any sculptor. Driving along the arterial roads of Cornwall you might think that all the skill and poetry of the people have entirely disappeared, but it is not true. The careful eyes and gentle cunning hands are still there when the right work gives them an opportunity. Of course, asbestos slates have already replaced most of the products of Delabole for roofing, and plastic tiles are now used instead of them on the floors. But even after Delabole Quarry closes, it fortunately cannot be covered up. Its lip will remain a good site to meditate upon.

Another reason for going to Delabole is to eat at the 'Cornish Arms' which is about two miles outside the village on the road to Tintagel. The proprietors have, happily, refrained from any exuberance in decoration. They have not pretended that the pub was a coaching inn, and festooned the exterior with painted cartwheels, nor have they exploited any association with smugglers or highwaymen which decorations spoil so many Cornish inns, and reduce them to something like a sideshow at a circus. Here the owners have concentrated their energies on their restaurant. They serve fresh fish from Port Isaac. Their menu is unusually enterprising, and the charges are most modest.

Both the legend of King Arthur and the myth of Tristan and Isolde are connected with this headland. This fact by itself is extraordinary: that two major European myths should be associated with one place. There are many accounts of the origin of the Tristan and Isolde legend. I would recommend *The Romance of Tristan* by J. Bedier, translated by Hilaire Belloc. Reading this, I noticed not only the parallel between Tristan and Arthur, but a similarity of both of these heroes with St George. We have Arthur's stupendous prowess in the field, and we see that Tristan, far from being a more romantic figure is, in the original, also accredited with the slaying of monsters, just as St George slew the dragon. All three reveal the same mythological roots in the unconscious. It is not surprising that after the Romans had pushed the Britons into

Wales and Cornwall they should find it necessary to create a myth of a superhuman king or general who overcame their enemies.

The romantic part of the Tristan legend can also be compared with the legend based on Tavistock in Devonshire, where again we have a king sending a courtier to act as his suitor and the complications resultant from the suitor falling in love with the woman of the king's choice.

Both of the legends based on Tintagel have given rise to a great deal of literature. *King Arthur;* Malory's *Morte d'Arthur* and the *Idylls of the King;* and Tristan has been the subject of more than one opera. It is interesting to speculate why these extremely potent legends should have arisen from this corner of Cornwall. The connection between the Arthurian and Tristan legends is actually reinforced when in some accounts Tristan is made a Knight of the Round Table. Though it is possible to discuss the origins of poetry it is not possible to explain it. Unhappily, whatever the impulses were, absolutely nothing remains of the creative impulse that gave them birth. At Tintagel we see nothing now but commercial exploitation of these myths. It is the achievement of the twentieth century to turn a poem into a bazaar; Isolde into an ashtray.

Be careful now that by keeping to the main road you do not drive through Boscastle without seeing the old part of the town which lies well above the harbour. This High Street contains some splendid houses and is well worth a visit.

Here are a row of buildings which were designed without an architect. Nobody planned them. Use designed them, local skill built them. There are no two houses which are similar. Some have thatched roofs, some have grouted slates. One or two have bay windows. There is no regularity or symmetry of design. Yet the effect is of a pleasing homogeneous whole. It is not simply a case that age has cast dignity over these buildings, nor are they pleasant because of the material out of which they are made. It is quite an exercise in aesthetics to stand there and try to work out why a row of houses like these are pleasing, whereas the new buildings at Widemouth or Crackington Haven are nothing less than an affront. It cannot be that it is the regularity of the former which displeases because a row of Georgian or Regency houses have this attribute and are delightful because of it. It is more likely that the reason is something to do with the intrinsic proportions. Today we build blocks which are shoddy when they are new. The sort of detail which makes for this shoddiness can be seen, for example, in the walls round some bungalows, in contrast to the walls round the cottages in the High Street. In the first they are of concrete blocks, sturdily serviceable, thrown up in haste and hardly cemented together, and certainly not pointed; whereas the walls round the cottages are of untrimmed granite or slate slabs: here no mortar has been used at all. You can see that every stone has been chipped square, then tapped into place, one row leaning to the right, the next to the left, producing a herringbone effect down the face of the wall. When all is said and done regarding civilisation and culture, does it, in fact, begin and exist in details like this? Indeed, you might say that an age could be assessed by the care or lack of concern which shows between any two stones in a wall it built. By this criterion the Incas would make us all appear savages.

You will find many old inns at Boscastle. I hope you will find them more hospitable to you than one called 'The Ship' was to the poet Robert Stephen Hawker less than a century ago:

We reached in safety our bourn for the night at the bottom of the hill, and discovered the hostelry by the sign which swung above the door. This appeared to us to represent a man's shoe; but when we had read the legend, we found that it signified the *Ship Inn*, and was the 'actual effigy' of a vessel which belonged to the port. Here we received a smiling welcome from the hostess, a ruddy-visaged widow. She then invited us to enter her 'parrolar', a room rather cosy than magnificent; for when our landlady had followed in her two guests, and stood at the door, no one beside could have forced an entrance any more than a canon ball could cleave through a feather-bed. We then proceeded to confer about beds for the night, not without misgiving, inquired if she could supply a couple of those indispensable places of repose. A demur ensued. All the gentry in the town, she declared were accustomed to sleep 'two in a bed', and the officers that travelled the country, and stopped at her house, would mostly do the same; but, however, if we commanded two beds for only two people, two we must have; only, although they were both in the same room, we must certainly pay for two, sixpence apiece was her regular price. We assented, and then went on to entreat that we might dine. She graciously agreed; but to all our questions as to our fare her sole response was, 'Meat—meat and taties'. 'Some call 'em', she added in a scornful tone, ' "putraties", but we always say "taties" here.' The specific differences between beef, mutton, veal, etc., seemed to be utterly or artfully ignored, and to every frenzied inquiry her calm inexorable reply was 'Meat—nice wholesome meat and taties'.

It is a wretched truth that by no effort could we ascertain what it was that was roasted for us that day by widow Treworgy, hostess of The Ship, and which we consumed. Was it a piece of Boscastle baby? There was not a vestige of bone nor any outline that could identify the joint, and the not unsavoury taste was something like tender veal. It was not until years afterwards that light was thrown on our mysterious dinner that day by a passage which I accidently turned up in an ancient history of Cornwall. Therein I read 'that the sillie people of Bouscastle and Boussiney do catch in the summer seas divers young soleys (seals), which, doubtful if they be fish or flesh, conynge housewives will nevertheless roast, and do make thereof very savoury meat'. The bill which we duly transcribed ran:

Captens		
T for 2	o	6
Sleep for 2	1	o
Meat and taties and Bier	1	6
Breasks	1	6

A few miles along the coast you come to Crackington Haven. This is one of the best sandy beaches for surfing on the Cornish coast. This attraction has, unhappily, reduced the cliffs to a shanty-town. None of these buildings was there 30 years ago—many have been built in the so-called planning era. The same mess appears at Widemouth, the next resort along the coast in the direction of Bude. The only consolation is that since our values are shoddy our monuments are unlikely to be durable.

Devon and Cornwall have few large stately homes, but they have several small manor houses which are little known but worth visiting. A good example is Penfound Manor at Poundstock, eight miles outside Bude. The house is first mentioned in the Domesday Book. William the Conqueror gave the manor to his half-brother Robert, Count of Mortain. It is probable that this is the largest inhabited manor in the country. The Penfold family lived here from before the twelfth century until the last of the line, Henry Penfold, died in the poor-house in 1847.

The house grew over the centuries as the wealth and importance of the family increased. In Saxon times the Great Hall comprised the whole of the building, though it lacked a chimney. The fire was made in the centre of the floor, the smoke escaping through a hole in the roof. Of this original building only the north and west walls remain, both of which are more than six feet thick. The chimney was added in the reign of King John when this amenity was first used. Inside the chimney is a small shelf containing a bottle which it is said contains holy water from the River Jordan which a crusading Penfold brought home from the Holy land. There is a legend that anybody who removes the bottle will have the chimney collapse on his head. It is, of course, possible that the bottle does contain water from the River Jordan, since there is a river of that name only ten miles away at Boscastle.

The window in the Great Hall is Elizabethan, and the original glass was there until the last war.

As can be seen today, the Norman wing was built to the Great Hall. This consists of the ladies' bower, or Withdrawing Room, and the Solar Room above, to which access was gained by a stone staircase. This addition was made when three revolutionary ideas entered domestic architecture: the notion of two-storey buildings; privacy for women; and separate rooms for sleeping. All three refinements were, of course, imported from France.

The Solar or bedroom is still known as the 'haunted' room in the manor. The background of the legend is that Kate Penfold used this room during the Civil War. She was in love with a John Trebarefoot of Trebarefoot Manor, which is some three miles away. Her father disapproved of the attachment, and on the night of 26 April the couple arranged to elope. They made their plans by exchanging letters placed in a hollow oak which still stands. When Kate climbed out of her window to descend the ladder to her waiting swain, she was discovered by her father who rushed out with his sword. In the resulting brawl all three were killed. This scene is supposed to be repeated by the three ghosts every 26 April, but it is fair to say that the present tenants of the house have failed to see any supernatural manifestations, though they have done everything to encourage them.

In medieval times a stream ran through the hall and the site of this can still be seen in the house. The purpose of this was that scullions crossing from the buttery and bakehouses outside would have their feet washed before crossing the rest of the house. There are several other unique features in the building, including the Elizabethan staircase, built in 1589 from timbers salvaged from a Spanish galleon wrecked in Widemouth Bay. This staircase was an early form of burglar alarm. Each stair is sloped in a different direction, with a tread of a different width and each stair raised to a different height, making it impossible for any intruder to mount at night without stumbling.

The inscription above the granite archway to the medieval porch is also of some interest. In the inscription 'In the Yeare 1642' both the *e*'s are carved backwards. This was a method used in the time of the Civil War to indicate that a particular house was sympathetic to the Royalist cause.

Evidence of the family's sympathy for the Stuarts can be seen by the fact that they planted a Judas Tree in the garden as a protest against the beheading of Charles I.

Penfound Manor is in no sense a stately home but I know of no building which shows such a continuity of living. It is small and modest, having grown gradually as the family was able to add bits to it. It cannot be compared to the ostentatious country seats which were thrown up in vulgar competition by the tycoons of later periods. The manor is not National Trust property, but is open to the public. One of the most pleasing things about it is the manner in which it is furnished and maintained by the present occupants.

Poundstock Parish Church is also worth a visit, especially for the Guild House at the bottom of the churchyard, which pre-dates the actual church, and as at Braunton was constructed to house the masons that were building it. This building deserves renovating.

The Parish Church of St Marwenne, Marhamchurch, is a modest building of considerable charm. It has a unique feature in the floor, which is made of thin slates placed on their edge, making a chequered pattern over the entire building. It is the only floor of this kind and most attractive. The church lacks a screen, and is short of pews, but still has a beautiful early Jacobean pulpit with a canopy, or sounding-board, above it, and a chair of the same period in the sanctuary. It is said that the pews at St Marwenne had particularly beautiful carvings

on the bench ends, but that they were all stolen one night by a neighbouring parish. The wide village square at the back of the church has a
continental feeling about it.

Stratton is one of those old Cornish villages which have been fortunate enough to be bypassed. Five years ago the old High Street was
almost rattling to pieces as lorries changed gear up the steep hill, but
now it has returned to the quietness it knew centuries ago. The village
contains an old 'clink' or prison, and the Church of St Andrew,
which has a Norman foundation. The tower dates from about 1400,
and the south aisle perhaps less than a century later. The font is
Norman, and a fragment of the holy water stoup in the south porch
is of that period. This church has many similar features to Kilkhampton
and Morwenstow. The present screen is modern: unfortunately
nothing of the original remains. It was removed in the Reformation,
and the Bishop of Exeter ordered its destruction as 'one of the church
ornaments used for superstitious purposes'. The people of Stratton
resented this, as they had spent many thousands of pounds on their
screen only 30 years before. The stock-warden's books record many
entries of sums paid to men from Stratton to go to Exeter to plead
for the screen's preservation. They offered to remove the rood,
'even the figures of Christ and the Blessed Virgin Mary, if only the
church might be allowed to keep its screen'. But after 17 years of
argument, the Bishop concluded the matter by sending men to Stratton to 'beat down the screen with axes and hammers'.

The Arundel brass raised against the west wall is particularly fine,
and in a window in the north wall is a mutilated stone effigy of one
of the Crusaders. The other interesting item in this church is the
east window which was designed by Burne-Jones and executed by
William Morris. The pulpit is typical Jacobean, but without a canopy.

All these villages are attractive and within a few miles of the seaside
resort of Bude. I knew Bude when it was a pleasant seaside village
consisting of little more than a few cottages adjoining the 'Carrier's
Inn' which still stands opposite the canal. But then it was developed; a
large cinema was built on the top of the hill in the best Babylonian
style of the 1930s. This cinema is now almost empty, due to a resident
of Bude whom I used to see in the town during the war: his name was

John Baird. He invented television. I doubt if Bude even knows he was a resident, though there is a monument on every rooftop in the town to him.

The small Parish Church of St Pancras at Pancrasweek on the road between Kilkhampton and Holsworthy is worth a visit, because of the extremely fine Jacobean pulpit, and also because it is one of the few churches which is still partially wall-papered. Much of the original paper behind the altar is now rotting away owing to damp, but in places the gold and red decoration is still visible. The church has the usual barrel-shaped roof which is common in Devonshire. In the porch there is another example of the tiling which can be seen over the whole floor of the church at Marhamchurch, where Delabole slates are sunk on their edges with a chequered pattern.

The small town of Kilkhampton is worth visiting because of the church which has some particularly interesting features. The first of these is the porch with the inscription 'Porta Celi 1567' carved above it, which encloses and protects the inner Norman door from the Atlantic weather. This door is, I think, the best Norman door in Cornwall. Its date is probably about 1150.

The well-proportioned inside of the church has higher roofs than usual, both over the chancel and the aisles. These are supported on tall slender pillars, mostly monoliths which, it is said, come from Lundy Island.

But it is the baroque organ which is the unique treasure of this church. There is a legend that it is the same instrument on which the great composer, Henry Purcell, used to play in Westminster Abbey, though this cannot be proved. But nevertheless this organ would have deserved Purcell. I have never heard a finer instrument of this type. Its tone is clean and the notes precise. There is none of the blurr or sentimental noise which generally emerges from organs. This is due largely to the excellent restoration which it received in 1958. Fortunately the Vicar, the Rev. Ronald Watts, is a musician himself. If you are lucky you may hear him playing Bach.

Kilkhampton Parish Church contains some of the best examples of woodcarving on pews in Cornwall. Two of them are exceptional. One in the south-west corner, and the other in the north-west. They were originally a pair, probably the ends of the priest's stall carved in the fourteenth century. One depicts a bishop, the other his minister. There are 156 carved bench ends and panels in the church. Not all of them are original carvings, as some were replaced by copies when woodworm had destroyed them. The carvings on pews in Devonshire fall into four classes, and examples of all four can be seen in Kilkhampton church. There are: emblems which depict scenes of the Passion; heraldic, showing the coats of arms of the local Lord of the Manor; scroll work, and grotesque, which have for subjects bears, serpents, and other animals; lastly, there are the emblems of trades. These usually depict mallets, wheels and tools used in the building of the church, and sometimes agricultural implements of the district. These woodcarvings are extremely beautiful, although their workmanship is crude, and their design often childish and primitive—though this criticism could not be made against the elegant and sophisticated carvings to be found on many Jacobean pulpits. The pulpit which was in Kilkhampton church was removed in 1860, but a sketch of it shows that it was particularly beautiful both in design and in the details of decoration.

After seeing Kilkhampton church you must go to another, St Morwenna, the tiny parish church of Morwenstow, a village on the coast.

The Rev. Stephen Hawker, who was vicar of Morwenstow, pointed out that the chancel of this church is not straight, but conforms to the tradition that the plan of a church should follow the angle of Christ's head on the Cross. 'When Our Lord said "It is finished", His head was bowed down towards His right shoulder and towards the right-hand side of the Cross. It is in memory of this fact that many ancient churches like St Morwenna have a chancel that points in that direction.'

Robert Stephen Hawker gained a considerable reputation in the latter part of the last century, both as a poet and an eccentric. He was born in Plymouth in 1803 and was vicar of St Morwenna and curate of St Nectan's in Welcombe, the neighbouring parish, until he died in 1875. He became a Catholic on his death-bed. His reputation for eccentricity is not based on that fact, however, but for the company he kept. The story is still told in Welcombe how Hawker would walk

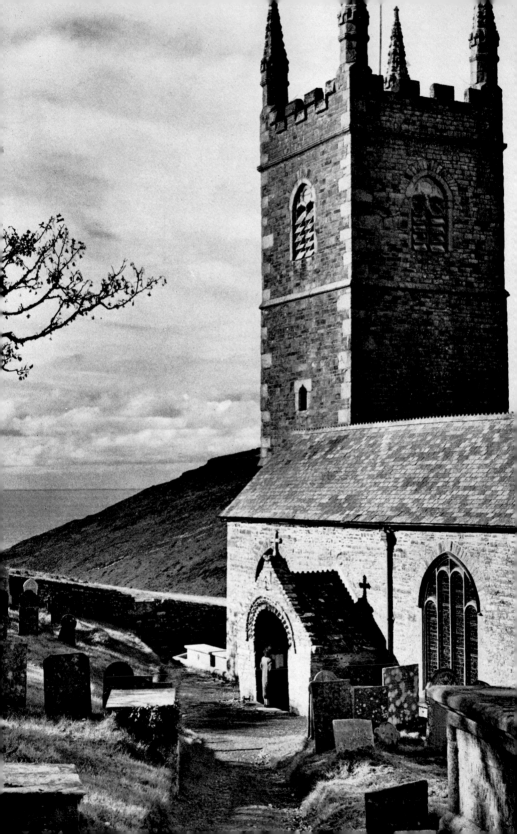

across to St Nectan's from his vicarage at Morwenstow, a distance of some five miles, followed invariably by a large black sow. When asked why he encouraged the pig to follow him, he replied that he had to have somebody to talk to in this Christian community.

Hawker was a friend of Tennyson and the latter stayed at the Vicarage in Morwenstow on several occasions. To my taste Hawker's poems suffer from excessive use of both the vocative case and exclamation marks. But his prose has not these rhetorical defects, and in several examples he catches the reality of this coastline which

> *From Hartland Point to Padstow Light*
> *Is a watery grave both by day and by night.*

In my own time I have seen at least four ships wrecked on this coast and carried a decapitated corpse up the cliff: on another occasion I picked up a severed foot amongst the driftwood.

Four graves for drowned sailors can be seen in Morwenstow churchyard. Hawker's description in a letter to a friend cannot be bettered:

Did I or did I not mention the wreck of the 'Ben Coolen' East Indiaman, at Bude, on the 21st October—crew thirty-two, six saved alive, twenty-six drowned? The channel is full of wreck—cargo—and among it corpses. Thirteen came ashore at Bude at the time of the wreck, some lashed to the raft: these are buried all in one pit in Bude Churchyard. This I do not call a Christian burial. We have lived in continual horror ever since, i.e. in sad and solemn expectation of the dead. Accordingly on Tuesday, the 4th, the message came at night. 'A corpse ashore, sir, at Stanbury Mouth'—a creek a mile south. I order a strong coffin and the corpse is locked in for the night. I write a letter for the Coroner, and deliver it for transit to the police: and there the 'misery' begins. Instead of a direct 'messenger' the Parish Constable, by a new, and therefore clumsy, loathsome law, the letter is passed on from parish to parish, through four or five hands, some at home, some to be searched for in the night; and thus, by this vague and tardy line of successional police, my letter only arrives with the Coroner at noon next day. He fills up, at my request, a warrant to bury, the inquest being incalled for; but being sent by the same mode, I do not receive it until noon on Thursday, and by that time the poor dissolving carcass of Adam, seventeen days dead, has so filled the surrounding air, that it is only by a strong effort of my own, and by drenching my men with gin (for bearers) that I can fulfil that duty which must be done . . . and a few days since I was startled at night with a message—'a woman has brought a man's right foot, sir, picked up at Combe'. This we have laid in the ground, till perhaps its body too may come;

81 *St. Morwenna, Morwenstow: sailors'*
graveyard, Stephen Hawker's parish

and now with twelve bodies still unfound and the set of the current always urging on the creeks of Morwenstow, you will understand the nervous, wretched state in which we listen all day and all night for those thrilling knocks at the door, which announce the advent of the dead.

On another occasion Hawker wrote as graphically:

The Wreck of the 'Margaret Quayle', of Liverpool, 1,050 tons, cargo salt, on Friday, December 4th, 1863—A cry at sunrise—a ship lying dismasted one mile off Hennacliff. Rushed out. Saw men on board the hull. Ship at anchor. In. Wrote a note to the coxwain of the Bude Lifeboat: 'Put your boat on her wheels, get horses at my expense, and hasten up towards us—putting to sea at the first feasible creek, to take off the crew.' Out again on my cliff with a glass. Saw the crew in knots on board, to and from: presently a boat lowered. Five men got in, pointing for Marsland Mouth. Got my pony and Mr Valentine his. Rode up to Hennacliff and then on along the cliff brink, side by side, as the boat rowed. Up and down hill and valley. Boat heading. Still upward, sometimes under the waves, then mounting them; on to Speke's Mill, on to Hartland Quay, allowed no signal to be made. Surf near shore too high for boat to live. At last watched her round the point and saw them make Clovelly Bay safe. Down to Hartland Quay, saw coastguard, got them to promise to watch all night, turned towards our own cliffs again. Dusk. Saw when we got near Marsland again another boat lowered; saw her staved on the ship's side, washed ashore at the mill, four oars, no men.

My own experiences of this coast entirely endorse Hawker's accounts. There are in this corner of North Cornwall some of the most impressive cliffs in England. They are too cruel to be called beautiful: too savage to be pretty. Great masses of granite kneeling into the Atlantic. Slabs of rock twisted in tortured strata. The buzzards wheeling over the bracken headlands, the gulls scissoring through the spray. This coast wears a storm well, somehow a fine day is false to it.

ELEVEN

Valediction

As I have indicated, both Devon and Cornwall are counties with a long history. For the most part it is accessible to the archaeologist alone and is visible only in the museums and in a few scattered ruins. Driving across the peninsula you will have noticed a solid farm here and there, and perhaps wondered why their walls look like fortifications. You may have noticed a Celtic Cross used as a sheep's rubbing post, or seen part of an abbey used as masonry in a bridge or acting as a kerbstone outside or as a lintel inside a pub, but from these relics you cannot possibly have visualised the great ecclesiastical buildings which once stood in Devon and Cornwall. Some of the inns, such as the 'Three Crowns' at Chagford, clearly benefited from the dissolution of the monasteries, but for the most part the past shows only in the place-names and in the narrow bridges constructed at the time of the pack-horse.

The great houses, too, you will have observed, show little evidence of their past. Many of them are inaccessible and have been turned into boarding schools, country clubs or guest houses. In the towns you will have seen examples of old buildings; often hidden away, sand-wiched between chain-store shops, or with their Georgian front adapted to act as a greengrocer's.

It is extraordinary how the past has disappeared. The sieges, battles and occupations have left so little trace on the land which suffered them. It seems that in Devonshire and Cornwall only the foxglove, the primrose and the honeysuckle survive from one century to another. All else, except for the docks and nettles, gets covered under within a few years. Even in my own lifetime I have seen how quickly the signs of the last war have been erased by concrete or weeds. So perhaps it is not surprising that we can find little trace of other periods when people were less efficient at damaging themselves and their heritage.

Though oddly enough, the most remote history of Devonshire and Cornwall is still visible along the cliffs and beaches and on Dartmoor; these granite headlands and derelict tracts still conjure up images of the Stone Age, and of the people who hunted the mammoth, the tiger and the hyena. There is little, however, in Devonshire reminiscent of the Golden Age when Sir Walter Raleigh, Drake and other navigators dominated the Elizabethan era. Except for Raleigh's birthplace and the copy of the *Golden Hind* sitting in Brixham Harbour, earning more in one week from tourists than Drake at his most piratical earned in a year, not a trace remains.

It is one thing to know that a piece of country has a past, quite another to see it, feel it or find any living evidence sufficient for you to experience a sense of history. I have not urged you to go into the museums. But perhaps you are lucky not to have seen signs of that history, for much of it was brutal. And you have been fortunate in this: you are probably of the last generation of visitors to see anything of the beauties of Devon and Cornwall before they are finally swamped by the urban sprawl of the twentieth century. Indeed, I do not know which is the more uncomfortable: to meditate on the cruel and elusive past or to imagine the progress that threatens our immediate future, when arterial roads drive across Exmoor and Dartmoor, reducing their grandeur to a kerbstone; when the towns have grown and Exeter has digested everything from Seaton and Sidmouth to Tiverton and Teignmouth; when Torquay links itself to Plymouth and Brixham, and other fishing towns abandon the last vestiges of their identity. Already Land's End is little better than a caravan site, and there is nothing to prevent Barnstaple and Bideford sinking their splendid rivalry in what will be known as a 'marriage'. If the population of England is to double during the next 25 years, you will have seen some of the country before it disappears. And it is not only the coombes and lanes which will get covered in concrete and despoiled by garages, it is something even more important: the identity of the people and the loss of their personality. Even in my own day I have seen Devonians forget how to bake, brew, thatch, weave or shoe a horse. It is true they can now decarbonise an engine and use an acetylene torch, but truly local crafts and tastes are disappearing. This loss is the most serious of all because it is a loss both of locality and personality. When all places are the same, none of us will have anywhere to go, and no longer belong where we are. The loss will be of home; and it is already happening.

Whatever qualities Devon and Cornwall have today, they have little use for art and even less for religion. Theirs is a culture where material comfort is the only impulse, and that comfort is standardised. There is no appetite in either county for excess, either for sin or virtue. Devon once had a tradition for eccentrics, but they have conformed or if not, people's eccentricities are too modest now to produce architectural follies or anecdotes which become legends. But I fear that the thing you will notice most in Devonshire and Cornwall is the lack of gaiety. In your whole tour I doubt if you will have heard anybody singing as they work. But just as there is little song in the West Country, so, too, are there few tears: perhaps they go together? We have found a way of life which is as cushioned from spiritual anguish as it is from emotional excess. A year or two ago a friend of mine from Spain visited Bideford and asked for some *vin du pays* to drink with his lunch. Unsmilingly, the waitress served him with a carafe of water—the whole range of individual and social experience has narrowed. We have found the *via media*, the lowest common denominator, and security is the one thing which now counts. The anguish of Tristan and Isolde or the heroisms of archetypes like Arthur are no longer with us. We are insulated, much more hygienic; even our souls are wrapped in polythene.

Yet it may well be that material comfort has always been the principal concern of the majority of people. The notion that everybody in the Elizabethan age had the spirit of adventure in them is a fallacy. True, they produced a Drake and a Raleigh. And our age has known a couple who have walked in space. But in both periods the average man was only interested in his average hearth. History gives us headlines which mislead us into thinking it depicts a general picture of the period. I remember in the last war, even at the time of Dunkirk, the average Devonian was barely involved. What worried him was whether it was going to rain if his hay was still out: whether his milk yield was up or down. The great historical events did not impinge. I suspect this has always been the case. I doubt whether more than a few thousand people in the peninsula knew that the Wars of the Roses or the Civil War ever took place. They knew certainly of the plague: they experienced the depression when the corn of the American Middle West suddenly flooded the country; but in the main political history has had little impact on country people. The things that have affected their lives more have been inventions: pumps that would make the daily trot to the well unnecessary: the design of a milk-float with a pneumatic tyre; the all-important invention of the tractor. Mechanical innovations have influenced the people's lives. It is silly of us to exaggerate the impact of politics, poetry or philosophy on people. These are minority interests: they have always been so.

Yet in spite of these limitations in the social sense, I have come to enjoy the essential sanity of the people. I can think of many places in the world where one might prefer to stay for a short time, but to settle and make your home there is another matter. I may have said some unkind things about both counties in this book: my permanent address partially redeems them.

The reason I live in Devon is something to do with the moors or the cliffs, because both of these seem to despise and defy humanity. It is their indifference which attracts me to them. In an age which is obsessed with human progress and materialism, it is a great relief to stand on some headland like Hartland and look out at the Atlantic which is aloof to both. And the gales we get along this coast make a comment with which I agree.

Index

The numerals in **bold type** refer to the **figure numbers** of the illustrations

Norden (historian), 139
Norman Conquest, 39, 112, 144, 169
North Heasley, 63
North Huish, 129
North Molton, 64
North Tawton, 100

Oakford, 57
Oare, 61
Okehampton, 96
Okehampton Castle, Church and
Town Hall, 100
'Old Mason's Arms', Sidmouth, 51
Otterton, 51
Ottery St Mary, 37, 52, 55
Oysters, 154

Padstow, 138, 165
Pancrasweek, 173
Parsons, 'Sporting', 78
Pasties, 28
Pawton, 138
Pearse, Tom, 106
Penfold Family, 169
Penford, Kate, 170
Penfold Parish Church and Guild-
house, 72
Penfound Manor, 169–71
Penruddock Rising, The, 64
Pentaun, 38
Penzance, 154
Perranporth, 23
Perranzabuloe, 161
Phoenicians, 129
Pinhoe, 56
Pirates, 83, 84
Pirin, Saint, 143
Plague, 131
Plumleigh, Captain, on piracy (qu.),
84
Plymouth, 21, 87, 115, 116, 129–32,
149, 180
Plymouth Company, The, 131

Plympton Priory, 129
Poachers, 89, 92
Pole, Cardinal, 41
Polnassich, 150
Polperro, 150
'Poltimore Arms', Exmoor, 37, 63
Pomeroy, Sir Thomas, 41
Ponies, 61, 117
Pope, Alexander, 68
Population, 39
Porlock, 60
Porthpear, 150
Port Isaac, 147, 166
Postbridge, 2
Pottery, 67
Poughill, 57
Poundsgate, 111
Poundstock, 169
Poundstock Church, 171
Powderham Castle, 45
Prehistoric Man, 38, 83, 105, 123,
129, 137, 138, 159ff.; **15, 29**
Princetown, 101, 111
Printing press, first English, 115
Probus, 150
Public houses, Cornish, 149
'Puffing Billy', 145
Purcell, Henry, 173
Puritans, 71

Queensbury, Duchess of, 68

Raleigh, Sir Walter, 47ff., 64, 83,
96, 131, 145, 180
Redruth, 149, 155
Reformation, 40, 114, 139, 172
'Rendezvous de Gourmet', Truro,
149, 154
Roads, 19
Roche, Well at, 161
Roman Catholicism, 40, 41
Romanov Family, 52
Romans, 38, 129, 138